HOLLYWOOD WAR STORIES

How to Survive in the Trenches

A Rule Book

By

RICK FRIEDBERG

Additional contributions by Dick Chudnow

Second Edition

ISBN-10:1500991619

Published by Rick Friedberg.

Printed in the United States of America.

Table of Contents

INTRODUCTION

Hollywood, the "Dream Factory," is a tough place, and it's getting tougher. The road to a career in entertainment is a rocky one. It's filled with ruts, boulders, road rage, hijackers, and amphetamine-amped truck drivers. It's a war zone. But, hopefully, by following a few rules, learned from others whose journeys have survived this obstacle course, this test of will and talent, you just might find out how to make it in Hollywood. Or . . . you could be Kim Kardashian.

To the entertainment junkies, film and video makers, aspiring screenwriters, actors, artists, comics, and anyone who ponders a career in "the Industry," this is a story of one person's journey through the maze that is called show business. It's a business like no other. Though there's truth to that old-time song, "There's No Business Like Show Business," the reality is not always as upbeat as the tune.

Tens of thousands of students graduate from film and video production programs annually. Hundreds of thousands of writers create screenplays. And that's just in this country. Who knows how many come from oh, let's say . . . Kazakhstan?

What very few aspirant entertainment creators and performers might obtain is a sustaining career that they love. But it *is* possible. It takes having incredible tenacity, perseverance, and, above all, character.

Most people in power in Hollywood began their career with tenacity and perseverance, but, along the way, it seems they lost all character. Some are as morally corrupt as a Taliban warlord. Others are as trustworthy as a Wall Street banker. Even more lack the loyalty of an NBA superstar. An entertainment lawyer friend once described movie moguls like this: "They eat their young."

In my hometown, Cheyenne, Wyoming, when someone says, "Let's have lunch," they mean they're hungry and want to eat something with you. In Hollywood, when someone says, "Let's have lunch," they mean, "See you when I need you," and there's no mention of a time and place to eat.

Hollywood is the only place on earth where *everybody* has a script. Writers. Producers. Directors. Actors. Managers. Lawyers. Accountants. Hairdressers. Pool cleaners. Clothes cleaners. They all want fame and fortune.

The movie business is like a closed corral: sons of lawyers; daughters of agents; offspring of studio bosses. They have no guts. That's why there are so many remakes and sequels. Do something risky and you're suddenly outside the corral.

I've directed movies, television, TV commercials, music videos, and documentaries all over the Western world. Some of my work has won awards.

But I never fit in. I didn't know I didn't fit in because I never knew where or what "in" was. How did it all happen? How did I think that a kid with dreams of making films could do just that without any relatives or friends in the biz?

Along the way I realized I'm still working because I'm used to overcoming obstacles – doing whatever I had to do to survive in the trenches.

And here's a few rules I follow for you to consider:

RULE # 1:

IT'S ALL ABOUT PASSION

If you audition for a role as an actor, test your comedy routine, pitch an idea to a network or studio, sing or play your song, or show your video demo reel, its all about how much energy, perhaps humor, and certainly passion you put into that effort.

A good example was Noomi Rapace, a Swedish actress, who wanted to play the part of Lisbeth Salander in ***The Girl with the Dragon Tattoo***, the first film in a trilogy made from one of the best selling novels in history. Being naturally voluptuous (which she was in ***Sherlock Holmes: A Game of Shadows*** and ***Prometheus***), she didn't have a prayer to land the role of an anorectic, ninety-nine-pound bi-sexual punk. She lost fifty pounds, died her hair ink black and styled it in a faux hawk, got tattoos and piercings, and forced the producers to give her a shot.

Having won their various acting roles, Mathew McConnaughy, People Magazine's prediction to be the Sexiest Man Alive, appeared in several movies where it seemed mandatory to remove his shirt. Then he lost almost forty pounds to portray AIDS victim, Ron Woodruff, in ***The Dallas Buyer's Club*** and, later, similarly on TV, detective, "Rust" Cohle in *True Detective.* Just the opposite, which is usually done with costume body padding, Robert DeNiro, got in character to perform as Jake LaMotta in ***Raging Bull*** by gaining sixty pounds.

These fine actors had the passion to win their roles and perform them so memorably, no matter what it took.

* * * *

Claire Townsend, labeled one of the top seven "baby moguls" in *New West Magazine* and the *L.A. Times*, was one of the Hollywood "gate keepers." She liked my first movie, ***KGOD***, a.k.a. ***Pray TV***, and we became friends. Formerly a Vice President of Production at Twentieth Century Fox, Claire was singularly responsible for Fox making ***Quest for Fire***. I was amazed. I asked her, "How the hell did you sell a screenplay with no dialogue? Monkeys grunting through an entire movie?!" Her answer: "It was the passion of the filmmaker (Jean-Jacques Annaud.) He got up on my coffee table and acted out the entire script."

Despite being one of the entitled "daughters of," with an Ivy League education, Claire started as a reader for a hundred bucks a week for a major producer. He treated her like a slave. Although fearful of him, she wanted to write a tell-all book about Hollywood swine. Little did she know that she would soon contract breast cancer and die.

Through it all, Claire taught me a huge lesson: It's all about passion. Crashing the Gates. Breaking the Waves. Making something out of nothing. Surviving. Rest in peace dear Claire.

* * * *

Reminiscent of the Emmy Award–winning TV series *Mad Men*, a New York ad agency creative team, for whom I directed a TV commercial, told me about their experience pitching a campaign to Procter & Gamble.

They had to show up first thing Monday morning, at P&G's headquarters in Cincinnati, Ohio. They entered a conference room filled to capacity with dozens of bland, white, MBA males in monochrome suits. They had thirty minutes to complete their pitch, which included PowerPoint charts, storyboards, and animatics—animated versions of their storyboards.

After the presentation, with no feedback or particular enthusiasm from their audience, the creative team exited the room and flew back to New York, where they would hear if they were successful and were chosen as the ad agency for P&G. To me, this sounded like doing a comedic stand-up routine to a convention of morticians, or auditioning, nude, for a role as a swimsuit model for *Sports Illustrated* in front of a room full of blind people.

Don Draper, the lead character in *Mad Men*, would have muttered to himself, "Fuck them if they didn't get it. It's the best stuff they'll ever see."

Think of yourself as naked. No matter how bad your body is. But be so passionate about what you have to offer that your talent and idea will carry the day.

Incidentally, the creative team, about whom I spoke, did get the job, without being naked. That's how I came to know their story.

* * * *

My writing partner, Dick Chudnow, and I completed a screenplay called *1775*, which attributes the Revolutionary War to a circulation battle between the British establishment newspaper, edited by Thomas Pepys, and the fledgling Revolutionary American rag, edited by Thomas Paine. Both publishers embellish stories about Ben Franklin's whore-mongering with his cronies, Thomas Jefferson, George Washington, et al. It was a parody of period places, people, and events—a comedic vision of history.

We met with two vice presidents of United Artists, Willie Hunt and John Tarnoff, both well respected and the only executives who survived the bloodbath of firings after the making of ***Heaven's Gate***. They had both seen and liked our movie ***KGOD*** and were comedy fans.

We felt we were in a receptive room. We knew the script by heart and could act the dialogue. We had them laughing their tails off. Here's a short example of a scene when Will Madison, the cub reporter for the fledgling *New Amsterdam Times*, goes to cover the Salem witch trials:

EXT. NEW AMSTERDAM COURTHOUSE

WILL walks toward the building, stops to catch his breath.

At the bottom of the courthouse steps, we see a group of WITCHES picketing, with signs that read: FREE THE SALEM SEVEN ... SPELLCASTING IS EVERYPERSON'S RIGHT ... GIVE ME SORCERY OR GIVE ME DEATH....#WITCHES NOT BITCHES!

WILL registers the protestors, then mounts the steps and enters the courthouse.

INT. THE COURTHOUSE

WILL enters a long corridor to the various courtrooms. He spots a GUARD and asks directions:

WILL: I'm going to the witch trials.

GUARD: Which trials?

WILL: That's right, how do I get there?

GUARD: Where?

WILL: The witch trials.

GUARD: How would I know if you don't.

WILL: If I don't what?

GUARD: Know which trials you're going to.

WILL: Arghhhhh!

Exasperated, WILL opens the nearest courtroom door, and a bevy of BATS flies out. He nods at the BATS then enters.

WILL: This must be the place.

We stopped our pitch after twenty minutes, feeling we were home free. Willie, relaxing after a final laugh, looked at Tarnoff, then back at us. She said, "That is the funniest pitch I've ever heard." Tarnoff agreed, and then Willie continued, "We'll never make that movie."

We didn't know what to say. She continued further, with complete candor, "No one at this studio would understand it; it's a period piece, which is expensive; and, although all the characters are hysterical, this studio was built by movie stars. This is a youth movie, with an ensemble cast, and they'll never get it."

We know we gave it our all because we believed in it so passionately. It just wasn't the right place to pitch. We later had it optioned by a major producer, and, even though it was never produced, we never lost our belief.

There's passion fruit, the passion of love (which you may or may not confuse with the sex part), and, according to Mel Gibson, the passion of the Christ. Use any or all of them plus props, trendy clothes and tap shoes if you can tap dance, and, above all, your soul. Because, along with that pitch, that audition, that song, that stand-up routine, or the video you show, its all about the passion you display that, more often than not, becomes infectious to those listening to you.

RULE # 2:

BE DETERMINED TO THE POINT OF OBSESSION

The most fortunate in life are those who have such an obsession for something—singing, dancing, writing, painting, whatever they crave—that they will do it, no matter what. Shows like *American Idol*, *The Voice*, *So You Think You Can Dance*, and their many clones exemplify this incredible drive.

The sign on the wall above my writer friend's desk says: "Singularity of purpose." Some people may call that tunnel vision. Some might call it an unhealthy obsession. But those people are probably in some kind of therapy. This same looney toons writer told me, "You can't perform successfully if you are afraid of failing." I think that's true in any endeavor, but especially in this business. Failure is everywhere. It's in the air, in the water, even in Starbuck's. One just has to do whatever they must to succeed. Rejection may be painful, but it's part and parcel of the business. You shrug it off, learn from it, and go to your next meeting. It's like a baseball player who commits an error. If the player dwells on it, he or she is doomed.

When I came to Hollywood, to become a filmmaker, I had a lot of hope but little help. I befriended an assistant cameraman to Haskell Wexler, one of the finest cinematographers in movie history. Politically savvy, Wexler directed the movie ***Medium Cool***, an inside look at the rebellious anti-war movement in the late 1960s, and he won an academy award for ***One Flew Over The Cuckoo's Nest***.

I had written my first screenplay, "Look Back Now," about an advertising whiz and a Washington insider who amass the best and the brightest from the activist 1960s/'70s and run a candidate for president from Central Casting. Although I knew no one inside the Hollywood club, the aforementioned assistant cameraman gave my screenplay to Haskell, who phoned me and said, "Come visit me on the set. I like your script."

With eyes agape, I entered the Land of Giants; I was invited to the set of ***Coming Home***, directed by Hal Ashby, who directed ***Harold and Maude*** and ***The Landlord***. It was a huge movie shoot in a period-decorated veteran's hospital in Downey. But it was nothing compared to who then appeared—confident, one of the guys—Jane Fonda.

Haskell was terse and to the point: "I don't know if or when I can get your film made. But I want to option it." I didn't know what the term meant. I just said, "Sure!" He went back to work.

Jane Fonda, Hal Ashby, and Haskell Wexler were well respected but, at that time, ***Coming Home***, an anti-war film about crippled vets coming back from Vietnam, was not on the top of the "picks to pop" in Hollywood. It was only produced because it was conceived by Jane Fonda, who was inspired by Ron Kovic, a paraplegic Vietnam War veteran, who wrote *Born on the Fourth of July*, which would later become an Oscar-winning motion picture directed by Oliver Stone, starring Tom Cruise. As far as she was concerned, making the film was do-or-die.

Although I still relish meeting Haskell, Ashby, and Jane—mavericks who stood for what they believed in and made a beautiful film—Wexler never called me again, perhaps because he was too involved in his career. I hoped to *have* a career, but I knew, since I had no filmmaking or acting skills, that a career would have to start with a screenplay. And the only person I knew to write it was me.

* * * *

If you crave any kind of career in show business, you'll soon realize that there are dozens of other occupations that pay more, that will reward you based upon performance, and that even have some benefits like health care. You need an incredible drive to write, act, perform, or make films; you need *luck*; and you need a willingness to sleep on someone's couch, wear a clown suit to advertise used cars, and do anything you have to do to make it.

Thank God, and Steve Jobs and the many geniuses behind the ever-increasing internet streaming sites. Thanks to Japanese technology, there are also ever-refined and relatively-inexpensive cameras and computer software that every kid over twelve is capable of using. Make videos; show your acting, singing, and comedic performance; and create ideas—these days, short films like these can be seen by at least your friends and family or can be uploaded to the Internet—which could, possibly, go viral and cause *millions* of viewers to see them.

And *that* may just be your salvation.

RULE # 3:

GOOD IDEAS DON'T JUST FALL OFF A TURNIP TRUCK

Whether you're writing a stand-up routine, thinking of a movie idea, or conceiving a song, good, unique ideas are not easy to come by. Some of the great movies in history (***The Godfather***, ***The Bourne Identity***, ***Election***, ***The Hours***, ***Midnight Cowboy***, ***One Flew Over the Cuckoo's Nest***, and ***The Lord of the Rings***, to name just a few of hundreds, were all great novels first.

Still others were based upon real-life stories, like ***The Dallas Buyer's Club, 12 Years a Slave, The Butler, Captain Phillips, The Wolf of Wall Street*** and the unbelievable survival story ***Unbroken.***

Although I've read numerous biographies of rock legends, like Keith Richards and John Lennon, I can't attempt to mention the hundreds of song ideas that sprang from the minds of the Beatles, the Rolling Stones, Bob Dylan, Bruce Springsteen, Carole King, Willie Nelson, and all the others whose songs have been performed by hundreds of singers for decades.

As a comedy writer/director, I find there are the most unusual moments in movies—especially comedies—that, because they break the boundaries of credulity, political correctness, and outlandish behavior, strike me as *great* ideas, such as Dudley Moore's one-legged messenger job interview with Peter Cook in ***The Hound of the Baskervilles****,* Eddie Murphy's tirade when acting as a paraplegic in ***Trading Places***, Peter Sellers's "Heil Hitler" twich in ***Dr. Strangelove***, Meg Ryan's fake orgasm in

When Harry Met Sally, Cameron Diaz's semen hair gel in ***There's Something About Mary***, the end credits sequence in ***The Hangover***, the nude wrestling match in ***Borat***, and Lloyd Bridges's line, "I knew I picked the wrong day to stop sniffing glue," in ***Airplane!***.

Even more unique: the wood chipper scene in the Coen brothers' masterpiece, ***Fargo***, the Knights of the Round Table riding broomstick horses while their "wards" bang coconuts together for hoof sounds in ***Monty Python and the Holy Grail*** and the lobbyist's discussion of whose gun, alcohol, or tobacco lobbying group kills more people in Jason Reitman's ***Thank You for Smoking***,

There are thousands of truly unique ideas in dramas, action films, and other movies. I mention comedy bits because that is my pigeonhole, and, to reiterate, these ideas did not fall off of a turnip truck.

* * * *

I attended a class called Murder They Wrote, which was taught by L.A.–based crime novelists Faye and Jonathan Kellerman, Sue Grafton, Gerald Petievich, Robert Crais, and a few others. Each novelist discussed their writing methods and how they came up with their ideas.

The final—and in my opinion, the best—class speaker was a relatively new writer, Marcel Montecino. Before he was a writer, Marcel was a studio keyboard player from New Orleans who had an idea for a story. The book, called *The Cross Killer*, is about an older Jewish cop and his partner, a young Hollywood actor wannabee, and upon publication it became a best-selling novel. It got Marcel noticed and allowed him an advance to write an incredible novel—a music biz/love story called *Big Time*—about a New Orleans keyboard player who works part time taking bets for the Mafia. It was later optioned by Tom Cruise.

Since he was a teenager, Marcel had only wanted to be a songwriter/musician. He wrote songs for twenty-five years and never sold one of them. He, unlike all the other authors in the class, had no idea how he wrote what he wrote. But when *The Cross Killer* came into his head, he *had* to write it.

I would never imply that, if an idea doesn't hit you over the head, you have to crawl back to bed and bemoan your fate. Conjuring up your own "vision"—be it a song, a book, a movie, a script, a video, or a comic routine—takes things like reading, Internet surfing, viewing movies and YouTube videos, watching television, visiting art exhibits, and attending concerts and comedy clubs. Someone read, saw or found incredible ideas that recently led to awesome movies like ***Moonlight, Get Out, American Hustle, 3 Billboards outside Ebbing Missouri*** and the masterpiece, ***The Grand Budapest Hotel.***

If you want to make it as a singer, actor, comic, or moviemaker, you have to keep trying, searching, researching, writing notes to yourself, and jamming with your friends until that "aha!" idea occurs.

And it will.

RULE # 4:

HOLLYWOOD IS STILL THE PROMISED LAND

Elements like union wages, location costs, traffic control and the lack of state and local tax and cash incentives have caused production in Hollywood to plummet. But it still is the hub of pitching, developing, talent management and deal making.

Long before I'd ever made movies, Hollywood pervaded my life. Everyone there had a swimming pool, a hot car, and a luscious babe. It was just like the John Cusack and Nicollette Sheridan movie ***The Sure Thing***, when Cusack tells his best friend, "All we have to do is go there. All the girls look like that and we can get one." As a guy in high school, that was music to my ears.

Lacking fear, or perhaps common sense, I got away with murder in high school. I took typing. This was long before mobile phones and iPads led to the two-thumb aproach to texting. I was college bound and heard one had to write a lot of papers. I picked up the ol' QWERTY pretty fast and impressed the teacher, a withered polio victim. She had difficulty walking up and down the aisles with her arm-cuff canes, so she mostly sat at her desk at the front of the room.

I took these opportunities to put the typewriter cover over my head, get down on my hands and knees, and creep up the aisles, feigning to cause mischief. They all laughed and covered for me because I was the class clown.

Years later, in Hollywood, I told my producer friend, Larry Franco, about this. I was working in New York, and I went to see ***Batman Returns***, which was produced by Larry. I was shocked when Michelle Pfeiffer, as Catwoman, said, on screen, "Yeah, little Ricky Friedberg used to look up my dress." A dubious but, I guess, "celebrity" moment for me. Despite being quite antithetical to the #TIMESUP movement, I meant to only solicit laughter.

* * * *

I loved high school. But I knew those years would be the best ones of my life in Cheyenne. I left my hometown the day I graduated. I went West to the promised land—Southern California; Hollywood—to attend USC. After College, I got married; my wife and I honeymooned in Europe with one backpack, and we wound up in New York. I had this notion that writers and filmmakers had to start in New York—one had to experience hardship to fuel one's art.

My first film job was as a production assistant for a TV commercial production company located on Forty-sixth Street, between Fifth and Sixth Avenue. Across the street was a place famous for its knishes. One lunchtime I found myself behind Dustin Hoffman in line. He was already famous for ***The Graduate*** and ***Midnight Cowboy***. He personified the difference between New York and Hollywood. He was so humble, despite the fact that movie stars are usually treated like they're movie stars, their lackeys anticipating every whim or need. Coming home from the set, when asked by their mate to put the toilet seat down, they'd ask, " Don't we have people for that?"

I asked him, "How'd you know about this place?" He smiled, "You kidding? I've been coming here for years. When I started out it was the only place you could eat a lot for little cash."

On weekends I borrowed the company's 16mm Bolex camera, commandeered some actor friends, and made a bunch of mock commercials for a demo. I labored over that footage, learned to cut "on the beat"—with the visuals timed to music. The company shot a CLIO Award–winning Pepsi spot in California, featuring blonde beach babes in bikinis tossing a football to tanned young guys with six-pack abs. My mock commercial was contrapuntal to the visuals they shot and to their music. It went like this: (Song lyrics from the company's commerical):

"You've got a lot to live . . ."

My video:

```
WINO LAYING IN A DOORWAY.
HOOKER STUMBLING IN HER HI-HEELS.
GARBAGE PILED AGAINST A TENEMENT.
PIMP IN CADDY DRIVING BY.
```

Song lyrics:

" . . . and Pepsi's got a love to give ."

My video:

```
SMOKE SPEWING OUT A BRICK TOWER.
JEHOVAH'S WITNESS SIGN IN BROOKLYN.
DRIVE-BY GANGSTERS DRINKING 40s.
GROUP OF OLD MEN SHOOTING CRAPS.
```

I entered the finished one-minute film in the first annual sixty-second film festival in Chicago. I was a finalist. But it didn't yet help me up my stock in trade. I needed to fulfill my dream. One Hollywood friend told me, "You can make films anywhere. But Hollywood is where the deals are made."

Many talented people—like John Carpenter of St. Louis, John Waters of Baltimore, Robert Rodriguez of San

Antonio, Richard Linklater of Austin, Alexander Payne of Nebraska, not to mention far-flung Aussie, Baz Luhrman and Kiwi, Peter Jackson or, most recently, Benh Zeitlin of New Orleans—are/were able to accomplish great work outside of Hollywood. But they all flock to Hollywood, home of the movie studios and television industry, because the power brokers beckon them with fame and fortune.

* * * *

At the turn of the current century came Hollywood's own "great depression,"—the dot-com collapse. The economy tanked and prices went sky high, which forced production out of film-friendly Hollywood to Michigan, Louisiana, Virginia, New Mexico, Canada, and even Romania, where tax and cash rebates were offered.

The beauty and authenticity of ancient Rome in Ridley Scott's ***Gladiator*** or of New York in Martin Scorsese's ***Gangs of New York*** or Francis Ford Coppola's ***The Godfather***, to mention a few of the many greats, offer the viewer the feeling of being in that time and place through astounding production, set design, and CGI (computer generated images). But it is also the authentic location of movies that gives us a visceral feeling—like Debra Granik's ***Winter's Bone*** and the way it depicts meth heads in the Ozarks, or Ben Affleck's ***Gone Baby Gone*** or Mark Wahlberg's ***The Fighter***, that lend us a look of "Southie" life in downscale Boston or ***Boyz N the Hood***, ***Training Day***, or ***Laurel Canyon*** that could only have been shot in their natural setting—Los Angeles.

Similarly, movies that are about the culture they portray, such as ***Slumdog Millionaire*** or even ***Nebraska***, can only be shot in the location of their story.

Expense is almost always the reason for shooting a film in a location not originally intended by the written material. ***Apocalypse Now*** could not be shot in Vietnam because of politics. ***District 9***, the under-praised, apocalypic movie used Soweto, South Africa, as its setting not just for lower cost but also for the aesthetics and authenticity of a downtrodden, impoverished area.

As is said in real estate, sex, and filmmaking: Location, Location, Location.

Much later in my career, I was directing a scene in an abandoned jail in Lincoln Heights, a seedy part of old Los Angeles, for the movie ***Off the Wall***. The scene takes place in a long hallway surrounded by jail cells filled with scary prisoners.

In the film, Paul Sorvino, playing the crazy warden who thinks his prison is inhabited by alien forces, makes his nightly rounds, detailing his paranoid beliefs to his summer intern, Moscowitz, played by Dick Chudnow, and how he's found the method to deter the aliens. Here's a snippet:

INT. PRISON CELL HALLWAY - NIGHT

The WARDEN darts his head back and forth, staring down prisoners and what he thinks are aliens. Then he stops short and looks into space.

WARDEN: You hear that?

MOSCOWITZ: What?

The WARDEN propels MOSCOWITZ through a doorway and slams it behind them.

WARDEN: They cain't shine their death ray through the bars.

MOSCOWITZ: Sir, I need you to sign my papers for—

WARDEN (interrupting): Lookie here, it's all comin' down. Remember that food fight, then Liefler got sick, San Diablo got hurt, and then you know what happened, we had a paper clip problem and then the pencils went missin'.

MOSCOWITZ (sarcastic): Pencils!

WARDEN: That's right. (Then talking into space) Well, you have penetrated my quarters but you have not penetrated my brain pan.

MOSCOWITZ looks at him like he's crazy.

WARDEN: And you know who it is? It ain't them commies, it ain't them geeks, it's the Masters of Mind Control.

MOSKOWITZ (sarcastic): Uh, huh.

WARDEN: But I got a test. They cain't stand music. A regalar tone (he holds one note for a long time as he sweeps his hand across his body), like real Amuricans like. Then wadda you give 'em? (He gestures a wavy hand movement and sings) Whoh, whoh, whoh.

He slaps MOSCOWITZ on the shoulder, nearly knocking him over.

WARDEN: See, I just tested you and you done good.

The eeriness of the location killed the comedy. The actors were flat. The crew was creeped out. The scene wasn't funny. Then we re-shot the scene with the identical dialogue in a prison set we had built in our South Central L.A. abandoned tire factory, and it was hilarious, thereby proving that a location can determine the intent and result of the story and its characters.

* * * *

Building sets is expensive. And although computer generated images that are used for location backgrounds have become much less expensive and time consuming every year, they are slow and still expensive. The huge "tent pole" films like ***Harry Potter, The Hunger Games, Planet of the Apes, Guardians of the Galaxy*** and the too many ***Marvel, Fast and Furious*** and ***Transformer*** films.

Find a location that dictates the aura of the story and allows the actors to feel the mood their characters would feel in that location. Think ***Midnight Cowboy***, the story of a cowboy hick in the biggest, baddest metropolis he could imagine, New York.

Yes, you can write, perform, and produce anywhere. You can even create something on YouTube or Vimeo or stream your creation online, but the meetings and pitches are still in Hollywood because the studios and production companies are based there, and that—and only that—makes it the promised land.

RULE # 5:

LIFE LESSONS AREN'T LEARNED IN SCHOOL; LIFE LESSONS ARE LEARNED BY LIVING

I attended the University of Southern California because, I think, when I watched them play in the Rose Bowl on television, in the middle of a freezing Cheyenne winter, all I saw in the stands were blond babes and guys in short sleeves, enjoying the sun. I had no idea that USC was the top cinema school in the country and had already spawned greats like George Lucas, John Milius, Robert Zemeckis, Ron Howard, and Taylor Hackford. But I did know it had the blonds. One of which, Roz, I met on the first day of school—our first class, at 8:00 AM, was Chemistry. Borrrrring. She turned to me and said, "Let's get the fuck outta here." Whoopee!

Even though I didn't go to film school, the most important thing I gained at USC was an elective class Roz recommended called "Monday Night at the Movies." It was an introduction to movies, hosted by *L.A. Times* film critic, Arthur Knight. The class showed new American and classic foreign films before they were put into theaters, and the screenings were accompanied by a question-and-answer session from either the writer, director or producer of the film.

This class got me hooked. I saw François Truffaut's film ***Jules et Jim*** and Frederico Fellini's film ***8 ½*** and was so blown away that I went to see every film both of them made before and after. I saw the lavish David Lean epic ***Lawrence of Arabia*** and Sergio Leone's spaghetti Western starring Clint Eastwood, ***A Fistful of Dollars***.

A pivotal moment in my lust for filmmaking was when I saw Stanley Kubrick's ***Dr. Strangelove***. I had a love for satire, having read John Barth, J. P. Donleavy, and Henry Fielding. I was always amazed by Kubrick's inventiveness and his ability to come up with cinematic firsts like ***A Clockwork Orange*** and ***Barry Lyndon***. But it was ***Dr. Strangelove***, a satirical farce about the nuclear threat, that set me on a course of wanting to be in the world of cinematic satire.

* * * *

Love stories, in my opinion, are even more difficult to execute than satire. The best ones, like ***The English Patient***, ***Doctor Zhivago***, ***Moulin Rouge!***, and ***The Remains of the Day***, all have elements of "will they, won't they," even though we all hope the lovers will fall in love. Others are about families keeping lovers apart (***Romeo and Juliet***), ethnic differences (***West Side Story***), class differences (***Pretty Woman***), love in the time of tragedy (***Titanic***), love between broken' souls (***Silver Linings Playbook***) and when love doesn't work out (***Up in the Air***). To sustain this unique brand of tension is incredibly difficult for writers, actors, and directors. It takes magic. A writer, actor, or director can research the hell out speed-dating, but how do you research what happens in a heart? Because to various degrees, it's based on life experience.

I spent my junior year of college abroad in Vienna, Austria. Coming from Cheyenne, it was as far "a broad" as possible. It was an indelible introduction to art, architecture, and classical music—a lifetime's education in one year. Upon returning to USC, I found that my brother was trying to make it in the music business. He befriended Cass Elliot of The Mamas & the Papas, and I accompanied him to a recording session of their second album. Running the show behind the mixing board was Mick Jagger, and Keith Richards was at his side.

I kept trying to phone Roz, my former flame and a Stones freak, but her line was busy all day long. Late in the day, I finally reached her. Before I could get one word out, she snapped, "Get the fuck off the phone. I'm trying to get tickets to the Stones concert. The first five hundred callers to KFWB score them!" CRACK! She hung up. Not a great love story. Because, like life, love stories don't always work out.

One movie that touched me deeply, because of its love story and because of its setting in Vienna, was ***Before Sunrise***. The beauty of Austria, especially the Bruegel and Bosch paintings in the Kunsthistorisches Museum, for me, with dreams of photography and movies, were *MAD Magazine* surreal—it was like packing a frame with as much detailed and multi-leveled imagery as possible.

Years later, approaching a higher point in my career, I sat across a conference table from Joe Roth, president of Disney Studios. He'd read my script for ***Spy Hard***, a James Bond spoof. Roth said, knowingly, "So basically you're talking *MAD Magazine* filmmaking here." He got it! My version of cinematic imagery. I dreamt of making films with frames that shined with cinematic images.

The masters of cinema pack their frames with cinematic imagery. Fellini did this in ***Satyricon***. David Lean did it in ***Lawrence of Arabia***. Sergio Leone did it in ***Once Upon a Time in America***. Terry Gilliam did it in ***Brazil***. Coppola did it in ***The Godfather***. Ridley Scott did it in ***Blade Runner*** and in ***Black Hawk Down***, and Chris Nolan did it in ***Batman Begins*** and in ***The Dark Knight***. More recently, borrowing from classic Fellini and Truffaut films, 2014's Academy-Award winning foreign film, ***The Great Beauty,*** brought me back to the visceral love for cinematic imagery. I later was blown away by the constantly moving and choreography of the camera in ***Birdman*** and then was enraptured by the on-the-edge of your seat, action thriller, ***Mad Max, Fury Road***.

In Vienna, I had an old Minox camera, the little "spy" type; I used it to capture faces that exuded pain, age, and despair. Vienna had a vibe so different from the beauty of Rome, the grandeur of Paris, the bleakosity of Cheyenne. It oozed the *weltschmerz* of its people who refused to face the twentieth century. In its museums, I was drawn to the lighting techniques of the Dutch School—Vermeer in particular was considered the master of "source lighting," which became de rigueur for foreign films like the soft lighting of Sven Nyquist (cinematographer for Ingmar Bergman, winner of an Academy Award for ***Fanny and Alexander***). Later, the style became popular in American films; we see it in Bob Rafelson's ***The Postman Always Rings Twice*** and Philip Kaufman's ***The Unbearable Lightness of Being***. This lighting and the attention to artistic detail make movies an art form one can only learn about by experiencing art, in all its forms.

* * * *

If you have relatives that own oil wells or office buildings or if you want to go into debt for student loans for the next Millenium, you *might* be able to buy your way into one of the major film or dramatic arts schools. But you can audit and even attend a class or program in almost anything at almost any community college, trade school, performing arts department you want. Either way, you also must travel, read, learn a foreign language, talk to people—force yourself to do *something* because you will, thereby, enrich your life. And by doing so, you will have *a lot* more fodder for those cannons you want to fire with your ideas for writing, performing, singing, and making films and videos—the ideas that usually come from life experience.

The most competitive but rewarding avenue into writing and/or directing is to become an writer's assistant in television or a director's assistant in movies. This takes demonstrating writing and/or film making skills and the willingness to knock down doors 'til your knuckles bleed.

In addition to the extremely rewarding, albeit most difficult path to your dreams, you can apply to join the Director's Guild of America's trainee program. You must be a college graduate and can do well on SAT-type tests and, although a small percentage of applicants are accepted, the trajectory to film making is quite impressive.

Almost every major university's film department attempts to place interns with summer jobs in movies and television production. They offer class credit and many are well-respected for their efforts. One can also apply for a non-paid internship at many studios and production companies. If you see an old film, with now-disgraced Kevin Spacey, called ***Swimming with Sharks***, which was based upon a very famous producer, you'll see the kind of crow you must eat as an intern. But guess what—you'll learn! Irrespective of the treatment you receive, the errands you must run, the demeaning tasks you might be assigned, interning can be one of the best ways to learn technical, artistic and political practices from those that practice them. You'd be surprised at how quickly you can learn tasks you never before witnessed. It's my contention that, if you are around long enough and watch intently enough, you can learn in four weeks working on a movie what you learn in four years of film school.

RULE # 6:

MOVIES ABOUT SUBCULTURES APPEAL TO AUDIENCES WHO DON'T KNOW ABOUT THEM

2012's acclaimed Academy-award nominated independent movie, ***Beasts of the Southern Wild***, is a cinematic look at a culture and locale most viewers have never seen. There are a myriad of films, screenplays, and books that speak of a place, a time, and characters whose subculture is so unique to the mainstream that, if executed authentically, an audience will be fascinated.

My first "long form" film was a documentary on rodeo cowboys, shot during Frontier Days . . . the "Daddy of 'em All." Frontier Days, the world's oldest and largest rodeo, is held every July in Cheyenne, Wyoming, where the population swells to 250,000, five times its normal size. During Frontier Days, Cheyenne is a modern-day Wild West . . . where *anything* goes.

When I was twelve years old, I witnessed a cowboy ride his horse into the lobby of the Plains Hotel in the center of town. The cowboy yelled, "Yahoo!" tossed his lasso over another cowboy who was leaning over the mezzanine balcony rail, yanked the rope taut, and pulled the guy over the rail to the floor and dragged him into the street. It was a scene you'd see in an old Western movie, but these guys weren't stunt men.

The competition for prize money was costly. Most cowboys couldn't fathom doing it for a living. But none of the competitors second-guessed why they did what they did. One championship roper I interviewed summed it up like this: "Ya do today whatcha gotta do today and tomorra'll take care a itself."

I interviewed a ninety-seven-year-old ex-circuit judge on the day that Neil Armstrong first walked on the moon. Judge Pickett had broken horses on the Wyoming plains before the turn of the twentieth century, saw the horse-thief-turned-sheriff, Tom Horn, hung in the center of Cheyenne, and saw fences, automobiles, and television (and with it, manned space flight) all come to Cheyenne in his lifetime.

What was most informative was Judge Pickett's explanation of why you had to break your horse: "There weren't no fences. There weren't no towns. Nothin' for miles. If you fell off your horse and it bolted away, you died." That's the origin of bronc busting.

Shooting from the photographer's pit, across the arena from the chutes, I filmed broncs and bulls coming straight at me. A bronc came out of the chute, bucked higher in the air than basketball great LeBron James can jump, and fell over onto the rider, crushing him.

Stuart Millar, a producer from New York (***Little Big Man,***) was scouting the rodeo for a movie he was going to direct, based on the book *When the Legends Die.* He sought me out and told me, "Come and see me when you get back to L.A. I'd like to see your footage. I've never seen anything covered so efficiently."

When I returned to L.A., I called Millar at his office at Twentieth Century Fox. "Get over here and bring your film," he said. "I'll arrange for a room." The screening room at Fox was huge, and I was nervous. My film was 16mm and not color corrected. I felt *so* far out of my league.

The shot of the bronc and crushed rider appeared. Millar yelled to the projectionist, "Roll that again!" He viewed the scene again then stopped the film. My heart was in my throat. What was I thinking, being in the Big Time, at a movie studio?!

Stuart slapped me on the back and said, "I want to buy that footage." I'd reached nirvana. I needed the money. Best of all, the footage was used in his movie as the climactic scene. *Awesome,* I thought to myself, *I shot that. And it's going to be on full-size movie screens all over America!*

* * * *

There are a slew of books and films about subcultures. You could write a list as long as your arm of movies about the mafia, ***The Godfather*** being the pinnacle. But even smaller films, like Mark Wahlberg's ***The Fighter,*** give that visceral feeling of being inside a subculture. Oliver Stone's ***On Any Sunday*** gives us an insider's look at the the NFL. The definitive basketball movie ***Hoosiers*** and the documentary ***Hoop Dreams*** both give you that desire to root for someone. ***8 Mile*** gave insight into the world of rap, ***Bull Durham*** and ***Moneyball*** into that of baseball. ***Winter's Bone*** showed the pathetic lives of rural meth heads and ***Frozen River*** divulged a sad life of contemporary Native Americans. ***City of Hope*** captured the dispair in the poverty, drug and gangster-filled *favelas* that surround the very venues that will were used in 2014's Summer Olympics and in the World Cup in Rio de Janeiro. These are just a few of the legendary films that give an audience a microscopic view of a subculture. Just as compelling were the two gangster series on Netflix, *Narcos*, the inside story of Pablo Escobar's cocaine network, the incredible mafia epic series, *The Sopranos* and, also on Netflix, the turn of the 20the century's gangster series, *Peaky Blinders*.

With my rodeo film, I knew I had something about a subject not often seen. Growing up in Cheyenne and filming my rodeo documentary, I guess I inherited that maverick mentality that only came from living in my Western subculture. And, with two rifles in the back window of every pickup truck in town, I learned that guns are as intrinsic to the West as fast food is to our nation.

When I was a little kid, on Saturday mornings, I went to the only movie theater in town. All cowboy movies had the same plot: rich big city guys came West, forced people off their ranches, named the town after themselves, raped the cattle, and stole the women (or vice versa.)

But what I liked was the TV series *Maverick*. The lead character, Bret Maverick, lived by his wits. He was a gambler and a charmer. Maybe gutless, more probably smart, he did everything he could to avoid a gunfight.

Maybe there's an explanation for guns besides the Second Amendment—something to do with hunters and gatherers. The man brought home the bacon, and the woman cooked whatever her cowboy shot that day. Strong women have a history of "shooting first and asking questions later" in windblown Cheyenne. My mother, Minnie, epitomized a frontier woman. The chuckwagon, the kitchen of our house, was *her* domain. She swore like a sailor and smoked like a chimney and was a born storyteller.

Famed British actor, Sir John Gielgud, coined a remark that's been quoted a thousand times: "Dying is easy. Comedy is hard." Despite that, Minnie was hilarious. Inheriting Minnie's sense of humor, I was doomed to become a comedy writer and, later, director. And like Bret Maverick, I believed that guns don't have to be scary or murderous. They can also be funny or, in some instances, the focal point of the entire script/movie.

The French movie ***La Haine*** is about a group of ethnically-mixed ghetto youths who find a pistol, which emboldens them. There was one pistol in their whole environment, unlike our country where there are two guns for every person.

In the frenzied British Guy Ritchie comedy ***Lock, Stock and Two Smoking Barrels***, a potpouri of ethnic gangs find, steal, are robbed of, and, finally return a vintage musket that probably wouldn't kill a Kleenex box from six yards away.

Even in comedies, such as ***Date Night***, ***The Hangover***, and ***Get Shorty***, dozens of formidable-looking pistols are used as leverage in scenes the audience *knows* are only meant as a comedic threat to characters who pee their pants at the thought of being shot.

Nevertheless, even though sociologists would probably agree that violence in movies and television has lowered our cultural aversion to guns, it's damn near impossible to kill someone (if that's your plot point) with a plastic bat. There's no bigger threat, suspense object, or accident waiting to happen than a firearm. Especially in the subculture of rodeo cowboys and their Wild Western roots.

* * * *

If you come from, spend time in, visit, or know of a place, a gang, or a way of life (think what Hunter S. Thompson went through during his time with the Hell's Angels) that is out of the norm of readership or viewership …

Jump on it.

RULE # 7:

DO YOUR OWN THING

If you're writing a screenplay or making a short subject video or movie, the only way to be noticed is by crafting something that is unique to your "voice." The many films that started careers, whether they were in film festivals or independently distributed, like ***Pulp Fiction, Boogie Nights***, ***Monster's Ball*** or ***Boys Don't Cry*** display the unique talents of their creators, who did their own thing.

Concerts, protests, art, and the sexual revolution that mushroomed in the late 1960s and early 1970s changed the course of pop culture. Independent films were spawned by the free spirit of the counterculture that had its most central core in the Summer of Love in 1967 in San Francisco.

"Do your own thing" was coined in the Haight-Ashbury, San Francisco's hippie neighborhood. It meant not following what your parents, teachers, coaches, or corporate America told you was appropriate. Therefore, free sex, experimentation with drugs, and revolutionary music all were part of the personal character metamorphose of American youth. Had there never been this explosion of art, music, and films, there would never have been ***Easy Rider***, ***Woodstock***, or the ground-breaking ***Bonnie and Clyde*** and the many later music-driven films like Quentin Tarantino's ***Kill Bill, Inglorious Basterds, Django Unchained,*** Robert Rodriguez's ***Desparado*** and ***El Mariachi*** and one of my recent favorites, ***Baby Driver***.

I took the movement as a license to legitimize my being a maverick filmmaker. I was going to make it on my own terms by making my own films and photographing my contemporaries in protest marches, love-ins, states of euphoria, dressing up, undressing, dancing, singing, embracing, kissing, strolling, and strutting. I craved to capture what my eye recorded.

Tom Wolfe's *The Electric Kool-Aid Acid Test* describes the acid tests that defined a generation. Many of these tests were held at concert venues, primarily The Fillmore in San Francisco. During these years, I got into concerts for free. I was on "the list" because I worked for the Hip Job Co-Op—a storefront on Haight Street where we found jobs for hippies, primarily selling *The Oracle*, an underground newspaper that advertised the concerts. Our windows were filled with the unique posters designed by The Family Dog, a group of artists founded by Alton Kelley and Stanley "Mouse" Miller. They designed psychedelic posters for all the groups of the period. Their art nouveau style lettering epitomized what Aubrey Beardsley's work did as well—the flowing sensuality of the women's styles and sexual freedom in the Haight.

Tom Wolfe credits Timothy Leary as the academic pioneer of the acid movement. Leary was the psychologist who, during the '60s, advocated the use of psychedelics to expand one's mind and creativity. When I was casting my first movie, ***KGOD***, I got a phone call. It went like this:

"Rick?"

"Yes." (I talk to everyone.)

"This is Tim Leary. I just read your script, and I want to play the Evangelist, Buck Sunday."

I was speechless. Timothy fucking Leary. This is the man who coined the expression, "Turn on, tune in, drop out." He'd been on every magazine cover and television show in America. Whoaaaa!!!

But I turned him down. I felt like I had just refused an offer to join the Knights of the Round Table by saying, "Um, no thank you, King George, my hair is in curlers."

It was my first experience of how fleeting fame is: Here was a legend of American youth trying to make it in Hollywood. What did he need show biz for?! I'd already cast the role, plus I thought that having someone on set who might slip LSD into the actors' coffee was not a great idea.

* * * *

After grad school at San Francisco State—I earned my BA from USC and went straight there—I set out on a career path in film production. I became the assistant director on a TV commercial shoot in Oregon, and I met Ken Kesey, whom Tom Wolfe credits as a major force behind the acid movement of the 1960s. He was the literary genius who penned *One Flew Over the Cuckoo's Nest* and *Sometimes a Great Notion*, and he was already known nationwide as the ultimate outlaw.

Although he worked in the film industry (and later was involved with managing boxers in L.A.), Kesey despised Hollywood. He was a large, macho guy with a major chip on his shoulder, and the "star-town" seemed to bring out the worst in him. Kesey realized that you may be a giant among men but that a Hollywood hero today is tomorrow's has-been.

With reference to the psychedelic painted bus his "Merry Pranksters" drove across the country, Kesey's iconic metaphor was, "You're either on the bus or you're off the bus." This phrase didn't faze studio suits—they never road a bus anywhere, ever. In their minds, buses were strictly for losers and maids.

* * * *

George Clayton Johnson wrote two seminal sci-fi novels, *Logan's Run* and *Ocean's Eleven* (both were made into movies), as well as the premiere episode of TV's *The Twilight Zone*. He was a full-blooded Cherokee, stood five feet tall, weighed about a hundred pounds, and had shoulder-length white hair.

George came to me with cans of film that various people had shot for him. He wanted to edit a teaser to raise funds for a documentary about a convening of futurists. It was his idea to assemble and sequester a dozen people, each of a different discipline—military, scientific, literary, educational, athletic, artistic, even con artistic, and so on—in a room beneath Las Vegas. He had an affinity for Vegas because it was the setting for *Ocean's Eleven*. He wanted to give them access to videos and archival material as research. The Internet was in its infancy and, though it didn't yet exist, he probably imagined a future with Google.

George's idea for his futurists would be to assign them the task of running Las Vegas, as a microcosm of the nation, in all facets of traffic, education, crime prevention, poverty eradication, ecology, real estate development—the works. One of the reasons he thought our collaboration pre-ordained, was that, as he told me, "I also grew up in Cheyenne—lived in the doorway of the Plains Hotel."

At this point, I had begun directing TV commercials. I converted the garage behind my house into an editing room. While tinkering with George's film, I "dialed for dollars" to get directing work. But before meeting George, I got a call from John Urie, who previously had given me my first job in Hollywood as an editor, and who had also given me an entire editing room's worth of equipment when he closed his studio.

John told me over the phone, "I know you don't want to edit anymore, but I got something you shouldn't turn down. You'll make nine times the money you'd make directing. I just shot a campaign for Standard Oil. It's a big job. I want you to cut it." "I owe you my life, John. Sure I'll do it," I said.

The ad agency for Standard Oil, BBDO, San Francisco, had to fly down to see the cuts. At this point, no Internet transmission of video existed. In between assembling cuts to be seen by the agency, I'd work on George's teaser. While I edited, George sat on the side wall of our driveway, adjacent my garage editing room, dressed in red corduroys and an orange T-shirt with a plastic portable radio hanging around his neck. I'd go out there once in a while to check to see if he was receiving transmissions from WKRP in Andromeda.

One day there was a potential conflict of interest. My wife rushed out and said, "There's a bunch of guys from BBDO, at the door!" I looked at George. He was listening to a headset plugged into his portable radio. I made sure George was stoned and lost in his music or *Good Morning Mars* and then told Laurel, "Bring 'em on."

I quickly put George's film away and put the Standard Oil spots up. The ad guys walked directly into my open garage door and convened in a semi circle around the editing machine. They were quite complimentary. One guy said, "Yep, we did it again. America's gonna eat these spots up like candy." They slapped each other on the back and said, "Now where're we having lunch?"

They walked back to their cars, never acknowledging George, one of the most innovative minds of our generation. To them, if they even registered his presence, he looked like our landscaper taking a lunch break, and they probably thought Laurel was our English-speaking Norwegian maid.

Though I lovingly jest about George, there was never any doubt in my mind that, even if he was slightly looney, he was one of the finest examples of man's ability to fantasize about the future and write it as science fiction.

I respected Tim Leary for being a pioneer. I admired Ken Kesey for being a literary genius, and I idolized George for having an incredible vision of the future. And they all did their own thing.

* * * *

Jumping ahead to the digital revolution, there now exists inexpensive, high-quality HD cameras, the most common (and still adequate) of which is the iPhone. Taking advantage of this accessibility and using your creativity, you can wrangle your aspirant actor/comic/singer friends and use several of the home editing software programs like Apple's Final Cut Studio or Adobe Premier and you can make your own videos. You can also play instruments and sing into any mini electronic recorder or the soon-to-be-obsolete iPod.

Furthermore, there are ever-increasing numbers of Internet streaming sites like Netflix, Hulu, Amazon. iTunes and, coming soon, Apple and Google on which you can show your videos and play your songs. This, to me, is the ultimate in "do your own thing."

RULE # 8:

MAKING MOVIES COSTS A LOTTA MONEY; GET IT ANY WAY YOU CAN

With the increasingly sophisticated and less expensive high definition cameras and editing equipment available to us today, making a movie is possible. Famed director, Steven Soderberg did it his year with ***Unfound***. And, fortunately, with the exponential growth of cable television, Internet streaming, video-on-demand, and mobile phone and iPad capabilities, there are ways to get your work seen. Before this technological explosion, it wasn't so easy. But I got lucky. I found a benefactor in Texas, home of wildcatters, corrupt politicians, and cowpokes who have money running out their gun barrels.

Jess Newton Rayzor II was the youngest in a family of mega-rich oil and land developers. His only function: to give money away for tax write-offs. Rayzor asked me to do a documentary on Hayden Fry, the newly hired coach of North Texas State University, which is located in Rayzor's hometown of Denton. To quote the President of North Texas, "Football in Texas is next to Godliness." That's an understatement. Witness Aaron Latham's *Rolling Stone* article on Odessa, Texas, the epitome of high school football and the basis of the hit TV series *Friday Night Lights*.

Texas football coaches and Evangelists are interchangeable. Coach Fry knew when he was on camera. He performed like a movie characterization of a football coach. Life imitating art imitating life. His locker room speeches were rousing and evangelical. After a three-point loss to SMU, his locker room speech was compelling: "It's my fault. I take the blame. We could have kicked a field goal and tied the game, but I knew you boys had it in you to win. We just ran out of time. I'll never forget the effort you gave and the heart you showed. I'm proud of every one of you. Now let's pray."

The documentary was well received. In the process, Rayzor chose me as his go-to guy for ideas he wanted to make into movies. One of Rayzor's wild notions was to cover the trial of his Ft. Worth neighbor Cullen Davis, another mega-rich oil man, who shot and killed his wife and her lover in broad daylight—your basic vigilante behavior in Texas.

Rayzor asked me to come down and cover the Davis trial so we could make a TV movie. The turning point in the trial, geared toward defaming the adulterous wife, was footage obtained from CBS sports. It showed the wife getting it on with a pro golfer behind the eighteenth-hole bleachers. Rayzor thought Dan Jenkins, a Ft. Worth classmate of Davis, who wrote about golf, told them about the footage. I didn't go for the trial. But it *was* made into a TV movie called ***Texas Justice***.

The first time I flew to Texas to meet Rayzor, his "man," a bowlegged cow puncher, picked us up in a classic 1964 Lincoln Continental with suicide doors. Just like the one in which JFK was shot. He drove us to the family home in Denton which sat on the highest hill above the town. We drove up an uphill, narrow road, lined with Cypress trees. I thought I was smack dab in the middle of the Cary Grant/James Dean movie, ***Giant*** or the more recent Daniel Day-Lewis masterpiece, ***There Will be Blood.***

Texas is its own country. If it were actually up to Texans, it would be. ***Giant*** was no overstatement of the kinds of people you meet in Texas. The famed astronaut James Lovell, an invitee to a barbecue at Rayzor's ranch to honor Coach Fry, drove me to the San Antonio airport—without a flight suit.

One disarmingly colorful character I met, through Rayzor, was the president of the Dallas National Bank. Rayzor was helping me raise money for movies. We had lunch in the bank's penthouse executive dining room. The banker, in a pinstriped Armani suit, had a diamond pinkie ring the size of a walnut.

Noticing me staring at his hands, the banker laughed, "Gotta keep my nails manicured for the rich ol' biddies." I smiled as he went on, "During the Great Depression, as a youngster, I hustled pool throughout Oklahoma and Texas." Referring to his manicure, he continued, "The first thing you did, before enterin' a new town, was bite your fingernails down and make sure there was lots a dirt under them. Ya couldn't hustle pool if ya didn't look the part. It worked most often, but I did have my fingers broken more than once."

We left the bank and drove along back roads back to Rayzor's house in Fort Worth. Drinking his favorite Pearl beer as he steered, I asked him,

"Think he'll come through with some bread?"

"Stranger things have happened, pard.'"

"He's a *banker*, for God's sake."

"Who do you think funded those crazy oil riggers that made millions?"

"Yeah, but they understand oil. They'll take the risk. We're talkin' *movies*!"

"Oil, movies, shopping centers. All the same shit to me. Just a roll a the dice."

I kept up my phone relationship with Razor no matter how late he called me at night or how drunk he was. I knew he believed in me and, knowing he had money to burn, I just had to wait for the right project . . . after all, if the president of a bank hustled pool to survive the Depression, I'd do whatever I had to to raise money for a movie. You gotta get that money any way you can. Forget your pride, your dignity, your aversion to working odd jobs no one else wants—the ultimate goal is to make the movie you want, and you have to do it any way you can.

There are now numerous websites that are dedicated to funding aspiring artists, writers, and filmmakers, the current favorites are Kickstarter, Indigogo, GoFundMe, EquityNet and a host of others you'll find on Google under crowd funding. You can sign up to seek investment in a play, screenplay, movie, book, photo exhibit, invention, and even art that you hope to be sold or displayed. Granted, just like anything on the Internet, you will have competition for investment from hundreds of thousands of subscribers. But, if you're successful in raising the amount of money you dictate in the time frame in which you need it, you only have to pay a small fee for these services, and it is taken from the money you raise.

What a concept!

RULE # 9:

NEVER GET YOUR HOPES UP HIGHER THAN THE LOWEST DRAWER IN YOUR DESK

Poet Alexander Pope's quote "Hope springs eternal . . ." sounds like something a poet would believe. Is there any craft more obscure and less appreciated than poetry (yeah, the words of Jim Morrison, Bob Dylan, or John Lennon)? If we, in show biz, didn't have hope, we'd have long ago studied engineering. But one can never get one's hope up over things that, once scrutinized, don't deserve one's passion.

One hope I cultivated was with my lawyer. He introduced me to a new client, Jack White, a songwriter/music producer from Berlin. Capitalizing on the popular craze of disco, after ***Saturday Night Fever***, Jack established disco clubs, put together disco bands, and started a music label and publishing empire, becoming the King of Disco all over Europe. He came to L.A. to get into the movie business. Forunately for me, the first place he went was to my lawyer's office.

This lawyer, like most entertainment attorneys, was part of the intricate spiderweb that connects *everyone* in show business. Though entertainment lawyers represent star actors, writers, directors, producers, talent agencies, and managers, few of them ever see the inside of a courtroom.

A piece of advice: if you or anyone in your family or group of friends knows an entertainment lawyer, latch on to him/her. Their job is to make the deal. My lawyer was kind enough to think of me when he met Jack White, because we were friends, not just because he could turn Jack into a deal with me.

Jack was charismatic and smart. I met with him and told him about a script I wanted to direct. He liked my maverick approach to film distribution—make the film first, then obtain a distributor afterwards. Jack was interested. He left town right after our meeting and told me he'd have the script translated into German and have "his people" in Germany read it. I couldn't sleep at night thinking that making a film was just around the corner. Jack White and whoever his people were would be the answer to my prayers.

In the meantime, after Jack left town and I was waiting to hear from him with high hopes, I was hired by Maurice Tuchman, curator of modern art at the Los Angeles County Museum of Art, to do a documentary for the museum and PBS. Maurice was well connected in Hollywood; he was a consultant to major agents, producers, and studio heads in buying art. Status symbols are everything in Hollywood. Buying art is as highfalutin a symbol as the moguls can acquire. I hoped he'd network me with his show biz friends. A bit opportunistic but it *is* show business.

I praised Maurice for his guts and taste in mounting the Ed Kienholz exhibit because the main piece in the exhibit—a life-size sculpture of a 1938 dodge displaying a fiberglass couple in the back seat making love—was very controversial. The doyennes of Los Angeles were outraged. I doubt seriously they ever got laid in the backseat of something so déclassé as a '38 Dodge.

Maurice and I traveled to Israel and filmed artists and artwork in museums, galleries, and artists' studios for an exhibit Maurice would mount at LACMA. Just before finishing shooting and preparing to return to L.A., I got a surprise call from Jack White. Jack asked me if I'd come to Berlin and meet with him and his "people." He offered to fly me there first class. Although I was anxious to get home, I told Maurice to go ahead back to L.A. without me and I flew to Berlin.

Walking to the pick-up area outside the airport, I heard a horn honk and spotted a tall, breathtaking brunette holding a sign with my name on it. Standing beside a long Mercedes, she asked me in perfect English, "Are you Rick?" I tried to impress her: "*Selbsverständlich*!"—absolutely. She got in the driver's seat and motioned me toward the back seat. I was hoping to sit beside her, but then I noticed, sitting next to her in the passenger seat, the largest, terrifying German shepherd I'd ever seen. She said, "Jack sent me to pick you up because he's running late." The dog looked at me menacingly, as if to say, "*Verstehen sie*?!"—understand!

It really didn't matter what I said or did; every time she spoke to me and I started to reply, the shepherd turned its head around and stared me down. I knew one false move and this four-legged menace would have me as a Rick Snack. I did find out that my driver was a previous Miss Germany and that now she lived with Jack.

We arrived at a modern mansion in an upscale suburb. I walked down the steps of the back house/studio and was warmly welcomed by Jack, who introduced me to three men in suits—accountant/lawyer types that looked just like their counterparts in L.A. I greeted them in German—big mistake. Europeans don't think Americans speak any language but English. I could have used this as an opportunity to overhear what they *really* thought, but, being young and far from crafty, I messed up. They immediately switched to German. I only understood about half of what they said, but Jack hospitably filled in the gaps in English.

After discussing the fillm, Jack drove me to one of the nicest hotels on the "Ku'damm"—what the locals call the Kurfürstendamm, the Champs-Élysées of Berlin. He apologized that he couldn't have dinner with me because he had to catch a plane to Munich, where the headquarters of his recording empire was established. I had an incredible dinner and took a stroll on the Ku'damm, which was modern and beautiful. I couldn't help thinking, *This is it. Fame and fortune are just around the corner. I've felt them—luxury cars, beautiful women, first-class flights—all almost within my grasp. I'm going to get to make a movie!*

But I never heard from Jack White again. My lawyer told me he'd opted for financing a pirate film with a more experienced director. It was a major disappointment for me, but I learned how it feels to be pumped up about something that may never happen. The film Jack made never saw the light of day.

Yeah, I got my hopes up much higher than my desk drawers, but the lesson I learned: Keep on truckin'. You gotta reinvent yourself every time you start a new idea, act, song, video endeavor, manuscript, or movie. But continue the creative process without hoping that, as soon as you complete that screenplay, stand-up routine, song, or video, the head of a studio or record label will immediately hear or see it and make you a star. Stranger things than getting your work propel you to stardom have happened, but the probability of *that* is not too much greater than winning the lottery. Have patience; the process is important. There's a learning curve, a body of work to complete, and a style of your own to display.

The product will come. And maybe stardom too. As William Goldman, in his brilliant book, *Adventures in the Screen Trade*, so aptly put it, "Nobody knows."

RULE # 10:

THERE ARE ALWAYS STRINGS ATTACHED TO OTHER PEOPLE'S MONEY

Dick Chudnow, with his college roommate Jim Abrahams and classmates David and Jerry Zucker, founded the Kentucky Fried Theatre in Madison, Wisconsin, across from a Kentucky Fried Chicken outlet. Then they all moved to L.A. and restarted the show—which was hilarious.

Dick's wife, Bobby, wanted to join the group. She was smart and funny, but she was almost too smart for her own good. When she and Dick posed the request for her to join the group, the answer from the other three was "no." Standing up for her, Dick quit, selling his share to the other three. This was at the point that the four of them were writing ***Airplane!***. And after ***Airplane!***, the rest became clover for Abrahams and the Zuckers.

I met Dick on the racquetball court, shortly after he quit the theatre and we became friends. I told him we should write together and make a movie. He said, "Let's include Nick." Nick Castle won an academy award with John Carpenter for a short at USC, and the two of them co-wrote ***Escape from New York***. Dick got a hold of Nick, and the three of us began brainstorming ideas for a film. Nick, a TV addict, asked me, "You ever watch that religious freak, Ernest Ainsley?" Ainsley was a popular televangelist. I snapped my fingers and said, "That's it—a religious TV station! K-G-O-D."

We knocked out a twenty-page treatment—spoofs on TV shows, game shows, commercials, and sketches that all sold religion. I had worked with a guy who was a born-again Christian who loved the concept and told me, "I know the group of theater owners who started the ***Rocky Horror Picture Show*** midnight showings by paying kids to dress in costumes, like they'd seen in the movie, and to come and see it."

He and I flew to Kansas City and met with the guys responsible for the ***Rocky Horror*** phenomenon, who told us, "You guys need a one-sheet poster and a theatrical trailer. With those, we can get bankable commitments from exhibitors."

I phoned my friend/benefactor, Rayzor, in Texas. A lapsed Baptist, he hated hypocrisy and was disgusted by the sale of religion. He read the treatment and said, "Pardner, this is hilarious. How much is it gonna cost me?" "Thirty grand," I told him. He didn't hesitate, "I'll send you a check."

With favors from friends, we shot a 35mm theatrical trailer and had a one-sheet poster designed. A guy I worked with took the trailer, poster, and script to American International Pictures, a successful small distributor run by the studio creative head who had to pass on producing ***Airplane!*** because it had three directors. AIP agreed to finance and distribute our film. It was everything I could do to keep from pinching myself. I was going to make a feature film!

Then I got a call from an agent, Jim Wiatt. "I just read your script," he said. "It's hysterical. Come in. Let's meet. I just made a six-picture deal for a client at Lorimar. I can get the script to him." I told him, "I already made a deal." He countered, "I know. Nothing's locked in stone."

I phoned my lawyer who told me, "I got a call from AIP. Wiatt said he represented you and was trying to squeeze them into instantly green lighting your picture or he'd take it elsewhere. I instantly called Wiatt and told him to back off."

This was the first in a long list of mistakes I'd make, by not listening to my inner maverick. Jim Wiatt had fire. My lawyer had a long Mercedes. His view was a bird in the hand is better than a sharp stick up your nose and AIP was my bird.

I later learned that it's important to have someone in the "club" representing you when you are working. They get the word out that you are the next pick to pop. I liked Wiatt. He became the second most powerful agent in Hollywood and the head of William Morris. He's out of William Morris now because he successfully masterminded a merger with Endeavor. The head of Endeavor, Ari Emanuel, the archetype agent Jeremy Piven played in *Entourage* and brother of Rahm Emanuel, now mayor of Chicago, thanked Jim by releasing him from heading up the new agency.

Although to Hollywood insiders the fall from the top is much greater the higher up you've ascended, they all land on a large cushion of money. Someone once told me, "People with money have everything else people without money have . . . plus the money." I guess Wiatt, like Mike Ovitz before him, never has to worry about getting his roof repaired.

I had a deal with AIP. We were going to make a movie, subject to one final meeting with the head of production (an old-time veteran), my lawyer, and me. After niceties were exchanged (nice being a stretch), we waited for the ax to fall. The head of production hesitated and then said, "The CEO of AIP wants just one favor . . ." I thought he'd want me to cast his daughter or add some werewolves. Or cast his daughter as a werewolf.

But it was something far different: “He’d like to make sure you add some pulchritude.” I was dumbfounded. I thought to myself, *Is that a religious thing?* He expanded, “Pulchritude. You know,” he gestured with both hands, pantomiming women’s boobs. “You know, bazoombas.” I smiled in relief; *bazoombas* I understood. “You know this is going to be PG rated,” I said. “It’s in the contract. We’re going to have a lot of hot babes in various scenes. We’ll dress them as sexily as possible.”

The next day my lawyer phoned me. He got the call from the studio exec with whom we had lunch. We had a go.

* * * *

The stories I’ve heard about how people have come up with money to live, to write, to record songs, and to make movies still surprise me. I have one friend that has edited two movies for a Serbian director totally financed by the Serbian mafia. My friend was loath to alienate *anyone* he met on that movie. The next one he cut, not for gangsters but so that the financier’s girlfriend could star in the movie, despite her obvious lack of talent.

I once beat my head against a wall and screamed, “I can’t take this shit anymore!” because some agent wouldn’t return my phone call. Fortunately, my friend and neighbor, who’s an entertainment attorney, laughed and told me, “Don’t you know they all go to agent school?” As interns and assistants, not calling someone not on your bosses’ lists of contacts is is the first thing learned in Agenting 101.

There are so many behavior protocols unknown to many of us writers, directors, actors, and musicians in Hollywood. But they are all practiced by agents, managers, producers, and all of their assistants. A good glimpse of this type of behavior always struck my funny bone when I watched the terrific look at show biz on the hit HBO series, *Entourage*.

First (this is learned by the interns and recent college grads who work for peanuts at large agencies): an agent, producer, or manager will *never* return your phone call if you need them more than they need you.

Then there are the less-obvious image points that one notices. Parking places are set aside at studios and agents' and managers' offices for VIP clients. The rest of us go through hoops with guards and parking garages a block and a half away from where we're supposed to meet these "suits."

The size of the office of any agent, manager, studio exec, and/or producer dictates his or her status level. If you are meeting with one of the "gatekeepers," the creative or development executives, you'll meet in an office the size of a closet with two chairs opposite their desk, one of which is loaded four feet high with screenplays displaying the cover pages of CAA, WME, and ICM.

My first agent, Marty Adelstein, liked my commercial demo and videos and couldn't understand why I wasn't far more in demand than I was. Then I saw the figurative lightbulb appear above his head. He told me, "You gotta come up with a story. Maybe you've been hooked on cocaine for three years and now you're clean. Dude, everyone in this town's had demons. That's what makes them interesting."

Marty went on to represent lawyer David E. Kelley, who created and produced *Ally McBeal* and a half dozen other hit TV series. Marty left his agency to head the TV department of giant Creative Artists' Agency and then began to produce his own series, *Prison Break*, and, subsequently, a terrific thriller movie, ***Hanna***.

I heard from people Marty worked with, who mentioned my name that he'd said, "I love that guy." He has never once returned my phone call.

Whether they are interns, assistants, script readers, future agents, managers, or producers, they are in the club. They meet and discuss who's hot and who's not while they exchange gossip about who's doing what to whom and, I imagine, how.

* * * *

My assistant director on ***Off the Wall*** became the golden boy line producer for Joel Silver, the producer of all the ***Die Hard***s. This A.D. told me that he wanted to direct but, although he had directed second unit on some of the biggest movies of the time, he didn't seem to know how to get into the "club."

Entertainment attorneys are one of the best links to power agents and managers. My A.D. approached one of the biggest power lawyers, Jake Bloom, who represented Joel Silver. Steve took out a roll of Benjamins, five grand worth, and slapped it on the lawyer's desk, saying, "I want in the club." A great ploy. This lawyer needed five grand like I need another T-shirt.

In the biz, there are a handful of superstars—actors, agents, directors, and rock stars who are accorded the highest perks: exotic cars, free trips in private jets, etc. The chosen ones also get floor seats at Lakers games: Jack Nicholson, ex super-agent Mike Ovitz, studio/record mogul David Geffen, Steven Spielberg, Tom Cruise, Penelope Cruz, Leo DiCaprio, Denzel Washington, soccer god David Beckham, comics Chris Rock and Adam Sandler, and a dozen other luminaries from television and the movies share this pleasure.

It's the highest honor, short of an Oscar, you can get. Each of the stars earn the high end of eight figures per year. I suspect they don't pay a nickel for the seats, which go for around four grand per seat per game.

This is a club reserved for Hollywood royalty. But I never cared for royalty. In history, too many were beheaded in the pursuit of more money and jewels than those kings and queens could count. It calls to mind a country expression: "If you can't eat it, drink it, drive it, wear it, or fuck it, it ain't no good."

Despite all these glorious tales of puffed-up egos, superficial protocols, and inhumane treatment of artists, you have to realize that if it were easy to overcome, anyone could do it. The best way to deal with it is to do everything you can to promote yourself, your art, your music, and your ideas. I really believe what one agent once told me: "Talent will out."

It will.

As long as you realize that, as previously mentioned, your hopes sometimes need a reality check. But equally important, when obtaining other people's money, there's *always* strings attached.

Deal with them.

RULE # 11:

IF YOU WRITE IT WELL, THEY WILL COME

Although there is great pain in casting, there is also joy. We had refined, acted, and knew every scene of the movie ***KGOD***, a.k.a. (later retitled) ***Pray TV***, and were in pre-production. Fern Champion and Pamela Basker, who had cast the Cheech and Chong movies, were our casting directors. I accompanied them to every improv group performance and comedy club in town. I was adamant about improvisational actors. They'd bring something to the party.

One of the parts, that of Willie Washington, a rapping preacher in the style of Jesse Jackson, was hysterical on paper. Roger E. Mosley, best know as Tom Selleck's sidekick on *Magnum, P.I.*, received the "sides" (pages of a scene in the script), came in, had the lines fully memorized (something every would-be auditioning actor should do), and nailed it. Roger's a confident, cocky guy, and asked, "What else you got?"

We had another part, that of Leroy X Washington, a born-again convicted ax murderer who goes on *The PTP Club* (as in Pass the Plate—a parody of *The Tonight Show*) to sell his book, *Ax Me About God*. He dances and sings a song Nick and Dick wrote, called "Born Again." Roger asked for a tape of the song, came back two days later with the song fully memorized and nailed that part also.

There was one part left, and it was impossible to cast. The movie's audition scene featured off-beat religious types: a rapping Hassid, a torch-singing sexpot, the Krishna quartet, a hippie flower girl, and the tough one—a preacher/auctioneer. We had dozens of actors read for the part. Finally, Dick threw up his hands and said, "Let's call the auctioneer's union and get a real auctioneer!" Fern said, "Just give this one last guy a shot."

Woody Eney was his name and he was awesome! In the movie, he wears coveralls and a plaid shirt. Chewing tobacco, he has a dog-eared bible in his hand. His scripted name is Reverend Hal Tramer. In his scene, he takes a breath, spits out a wad of tobacco, and starts to preach:

```
TRAMER: And the Lord sayeth unto
his disciples, "Giveth your first
born unto the Lord and be
plentiful and multiply." But they
couldn't multiply 'cause they
hadn't learned simple addition
yet. So they begot. They begot
whenever they could.
                (faster)
And unto them Shem, the father of
all the children of Eber, the
brother of Japeth the Elder, even
unto him were children born.
              (faster yet)
And Eber begat Salah and Salah
begat Obal.
             (even faster)
And Obal begat Sheba and Jobab
and Jobab begat Samuel and Sanuel
begat Claude and Claude begat Bee
Bee and Bee Bee begat and forgot
to begot so she hopped to the hop
doing the bibbity bobbity boo.
              (auctioning)
```

I got a boo, I got a bop, I got a—

DIRECTOR (V.O. from booth): Cut!

TRAMER:I got a cut. Do I hear another cut

DIRECTOR: CUT!!!

TRAMER: I got another cut. I got two cuts, do I hear three—

DIRECTOR: Would you please leave the stage!

TRAMER: I gotta leave the stage. I gotta leave the stage once. I gotta leave the stage twice. I gotta leave the stage three times. Gone! I'm off the stage.

The entire cast of ***KGOD*** brought something extra to their scenes. My belief is that if you craft unique characters and terrific dialogue, actors will want to play the parts.

****

Of course, there's always the downside: showing "dailies." Dailies are the film shot each day and they are viewed by studio executives. It is rare for filmmakers to watch dailies with the suits because they are too busy shooting their movies, but sometimes they have to.

I only had to sit through dailies with the studio twice. Both times ripped my guts out. The first time we viewed a scene in which four guys, in Hare Krishna saffron robes and bald wigs, sing a barbershop quartet song called "I love my God," written by Nick and Dick and choreographed by Michael Peters, who went on to fame with Michael Jackson's music video for "Thriller." One of the Krishnas couldn't lip sync. I was used to shooting three takes and moving on. This one went fifty-four. You could hear a pin drop in the screening room. If Dr. Kevorkian was still alive, I would have requested his services.

The other time I had to do this show-and-tell was for the opening exhortation scene. The character Marvin Fleece, played by Dabney Coleman, inspires the assembled crew of the tiny country TV station KRUD to broadcast religion. Because he improvised, he was always in a different place in the set. To make sure I could edit this scene, I had to shoot reaction shots from the other actors. Endless.

The scene takes place in the conference room of dilapidated 300-watt local TV station called KRUD in mythical San Poquito. All the staff of the station file into the conference room to hear the bad news:

```
INT. CONFERENCE ROOM - KRUD - DAY

MILLIE (the owner) stands to address the
crowd, clears her throat:

      MILLIE: As you all know, we've
      had a little cash flow problem
      lately.

      AD LIBS: Yeah, I haven't been
      paid in weeks.

      MILLIE: But now we're in deep
      shit (lifts stack of bills). The
      rent's two months overdue. The
      FCC licensing fee was due last
      week (raises computer printout).
      Worst of all, our ratings are no
      longer . . . rated.

She tosses the papers back onto her desk.
```

MILLIE: We got, at most, a month. A month, provided we *do* something.

She glances at MARVIN, who preens.

MILLIE: So I want you all to meet an old friend of mine who has graciously consented to help us. Ladies and gentlemen, Marvin Fleece.

MARVIN rises, smiles benevolently. He begins to pace.

MARVIN: Friends. And I'm sure you'll all become my friends. As bleak a picture as Millie here paints, I can assure you it's much worse than that.

GASPS of horror.

MARVIN: But I don't want you all to despair. Because I truly believe there is an answer here.

PEGGY the intern and FLETCHER, MILLIE's son, exchange a positive look.

MARVIN: You see, I believe that for every drop of rain that falls, a little tree will grow..

Now they exchange a puzzled look.

MARVIN: And I see a magnificent tree growing from the brambles of this station. (Dramatic pause) How, you ask?

FRED, the news/weather anchor, holds a ventriloquist's DUMMY on his lap. The DUMMY starts to open his mouth, but FRED covers the DUMMY's mouth.

MARVIN: By giving people what they want.

ALICE looks to FRED with a questioning look.

MARVIN: By giving people what they need. By giving them what their hearts and their minds are crying out for.

FRED looks back at ALICE and nods his head—this sounds good.

MARVIN: And what are they crying out for?

Everyone is nonplussed but excited in anticipation.

MARVIN: Salvation.

ALICE looks bewildered and silently mouths: "Salvation?"

MARVIN: That's right. Salvation. And when you think of salvation, what do you think of?

The DUMMY starts to open its mouth again, and again FRED covers it.

MARVIN: You think of God. God, almighty. That's what the people want. That's what the people need, and that's what we're going to give them!

MARCHING MUSIC starts to play underneath the dialogue.

MARVIN: We are going to create brand new programs. New programs that'll attract new viewers. And new viewers'll attract new sponsors!

The crowd is starting to buy it.

MARVIN: Let all those other TV stations give away cars. Cars and them crummy little Jap TV sets. But they will never compete with us. Because we are giving away the Word of God!

The crowd is jacked up.

MARVIN: Each and every one of you is going to go out there and spread His word upon this great land. Now get out there and get 'em!!!!

CHURCH ORGAN ROCK MUSIC adds punctuation as the staff files out of the conference room, jacked up.

The last day of the shoot was the biggest. The scene showed an evangelist rousing the crowd at an abandoned drive-in movie theater. Charlie Haid (*Hill Street Blues*) plays Buck Sunday, a showman Evangelist. He was accompanied on piano by Cajun blues singer Dr. John and, with his choir, they sang "Gimme Your Money," a kick-ass gospel tune Nick, Dick, and I wrote, with comic lyrics about what would happen if people didn't give all their cash to God. The scene starts with an establishing shot of the marquee at a drive-in move theatre: BUCK SUNDAY – The Mobile Church of God.

Following a line of cars entering the drive-in's parking lot, the camera reveals a huge crowd going wild as Buck glides to center stage, takes a mic off the stand, and begins to preach:

BUCK: You know, people ask me, they ask me, "Buck," they ask, "Is God dead?" And I answer and I say, "Noooo, God is not dead. He's in intensive care. He's sick. He's sick and tired of people making flimsy excuses for not emptying their wallets for Him. And he wants you to do it today, because tomorrow you may be dead and not able to go to the bank."

CROWD AD LIBS: Tell'em, Buck.

BUCK: So you ask me, "Buck," you ask, "How can I get to God's Heaven?" And I answer and I say, "It's not easy to get to God's heaven." And they ask me, "Can I get to God's heaven by doing good deeds?"

CROWD AD LIBS: "Yes Lord."

BUCK: "The only way to get to God's heaven is by doing the hardest thing there is to do. The hardest thing there is to do is to give every single penny you have to God. That's what's hard.

That's what hurts, and that's
what Gawwwd wants you to do."

CROWD (yells): HALLELUJAH!

Thunderous CHEERS.

BUCK: "Now I want to introduce to
you, and to the Man upstairs, our
special guest: Dr. John and the
Holey Moley Singers."

Incredible APPLAUSE as a white grand piano is rolled on stage followed by a chorus in purple choir robes. DR. JOHN strikes a CHORD. BUCK fades off stage as DR. JOHN plays and sings:

Once there was a man,
Didn't give us any money.
Left his checkbook at home.
Couldn't get to the bank on time
on Saturday.

So one day he walked 'cross
the street. Foot of God came
down and he tripped and stumbled
and fell in front of a truck
and died in the emergency room.

So what can you do if you don't
wanna end up like this guy?
Didn't give any money and ended
up dead.

What do you do-ooh-ooh.
What do you do-ooh-ooh.

BACK-UP SINGERS: *What do you do-*
ooh-ooh.

Give me your watch.

Give me your ring.

Give me your car, your truck, the mortgage on your home.

Let's have some bucks.
We'll take a check.
We'll take a money order
or a credit card.

Give me your stocks.
Give me your bonds.
Remember its going to the
Man up above.

BUCK runs back on stage with a wireless hand mic: "And remember, it's all tax deductible." Then he glides back off stage as DR. JOHN continues:

So dig real deep.
It's not enough.
Just give it all and
wash away your sins.
Gimme, gimme, gimme, gimme
all that you got. For Him.

BUCK, once again, rushes on with his hand mic: "We take Master Card, Visa, and American Express."

As DR. JOHN's song continues, we see USHERS, carrying velvet-covered garbage cans (tied between poles like you sometimes see pallbearers using to carry a casket), glide down the aisles as people in cars toss money, jewelry, and electronic goods into the cans.

The roller blading CARHOPS deliver wine and wafers. Their silver trays become laden with cash, credit cards, checks, and money orders.

Although they were terrific, I didn't have to watch these dailies with studio execs. But watching them with people who don't exactly know how they will be edited together is like swimming with sharks without a steel cage around you. Don't do it! Get stuck in traffic. Feign an epileptic fit. Tell them you have a communicable, potentially fatal disease that is infectious for up to however many shooting days you have left.

Above all, craft, try out, refine and believe in your material because if you do, an actor or singer or dancer will want to perform it. And if they like it that much, they'll do an awesome job and the audience will respond accordingly.

If you'd like to see the auctioneer's monologue, visit:

https://www.youtube.com/watch?v=_8bMD4FnW6c

If you'd like to see Buck Sunday and Dr John, visit:

https://www.youtube.com/watch?v=J0L3IJCEq-8

RULE # 12:

BOOK YOUR NEXT JOB BEFORE THE STAR OR THE STUDIO EXEC CROAKS

Cocaine came to Hollywood like a monsoon to Mumbai. The prop guy had a stash in his prop kit. It seemed like the crew on ***KGOD*** had an unnatural need for "props." While setting up for our shoot at the drive-in, I noticed a few musicians and actors exiting their trailers—they had been "rehearsing"—and wiping their noses. This was summer, not exactly flu season.

But Dick Chudnow had left his wife before shooting ***KGOD*** and was living on the couch in our office, so he was depressed and needed some "cheering up." The studio head asked for "pulchritude," and we cast some pretty sexy extras.

Cocaine or no cocaine, it was now the moment of truth. There were a half dozen hot extras, in skimpy shorts, on roller skates. I called one of them over and introduced her. "This is Dick Chudnow, our *producer*," I smiled, lying through my teeth, "You do know he discovered Madonna?" She smiled at him, "Really?" and sidled up to him, like a cat ready to purr. felt he was home free. Yeah, this was sexist and I now realize, perhaps inappropriate. But it was a time in which men were less sensitive to objectification of women. Nevertheless, I turned and rushed to the "set," the stage below the movie screen.

We had a PA system so that Charlie Haid and Dr. John's voices would echo into the crowd. Charlie had a question about the monologue Dick wrote. Assistant director Larry Franco (the one who put my name in

Batman Returns) got on the PA mic: "Dick. Dick Chudnow. Chudnow. You're needed on the set. Dick Chudnow!" I smiled to myself, thinking, "The monologue is just fine."

After ***KGOD*** was finished, my agent, Jane Sindell, who later produced ***Pleasantville*** and ***Seabiscuit***, set me up with Amy Ephron, the youngest sister of the famed family of comedy writers. Amy, an executive at Warner Brothers Studios, liked ***KGOD***. She called me in to meet John Veitch, head of production. They had optioned the rights to *Alley Oop*, a comic strip about a super-dumb caveman who is always getting in trouble. They wanted John Belushi to star in it.

This was the day of the academy awards. Mid-meeting, the side door to the office burst open. Through this door flew a hefty young man dressed in a tux. It was the creative president of the studio, with his bow tie loose. He was so coked up, his nose was running. He blurted out, "Anyone here know how to tie a bow tie?" Amy got up and tied his tie. He spun on his heels and returned to his office. This was a meeting ender. I guess Amy and Veitch were embarrassed. I didn't direct *Alley Oop*. Neither did anyone else. Belushi was dead of a cocaine overdose just months after that. This studio head died a year later. He was quite overweight, but, in that period of time, he may have also done a lotta coke.

Six months later, ***KGOD***, my first feature, was in the can. After months of hoping. Months of preparation, during which one of our production designers died of an overdose, making it three deaths from cocaine abuse. But that was their choice, and although I did eventually get another movie, I should have booked one as soon as the buzz over ***KGOD*** began. Though, with the rampant use of cocaine, it might have been just an ambient drug buzz in a lot of heads.

Use this as a lesson. Think about that next performance, audition, idea, screenplay or movie offer *before* you finish what's in front of you. You never know from where or when your next gig's coming.

Be pro active.

RULE # 13:

NO SIX PEOPLE LAUGH AT THE SAME JOKE

Growing up in Cheyenne and making a documentary on rodeo riders, I learned a lot about cowboys. Directing comedy television and movies I learned a bit about comics. Cowboys and comics have a lot in common: Cowboys don't respect people who haven't faced danger. Comedy people don't respect people who haven't failed at getting laughs. Cowboys know how to handle hostile hombres. Comedy people learn how to handle hecklers. Above all, comedy people and cowboys don't like being where they're not welcome.

I learned this well—while searching for a movie-making opportunity after we finished ***KGOD***—in the Universal Studios' executive building, called the Black Tower. On the top, penthouse floor were four gigantic offices: one for the CEO, legendary ex-agent Lew Wasserman; across from him, President of Production Ned Tanen; on the other side of the huge, empty "bull pen" Head of Business Affairs, Sid Sheinberg; and opposite Sheinberg, the comptroller, who's name I never knew. Does anyone know a comptroller's name? Does anyone know what they do? The word does have "troll" in it . . . I imagine it has something to do with that.

The floor had huge authentic Persian rugs and Ming vases. Each office had an antechamber for the assistant/secretary. The only sound you heard was faint: a computer keyboard, a ringing telephone, both of them so muted you could hardly hear them from two feet away. You even had to *think* quietly.

At the time, Universal was known as *the* place to do comedies. They had such success with ***Animal House, Blues Brothers*** and ***The Jerk***, that they had a lock on Saturday Night Live actors. We thought we were coming to the best place to make another comedy movie. Dick Chudnow and I were set to meet with Ned Tanen, who had seen and liked ***KGOD***.

Chudnow and I nervously awaited our turn while pacing across a carpet lightly so as not to disturb the funereal silence or leave a shoe impression in the lavish rug. Both of us knew without stating it: This is *wrong*. There is no comedy vibe here. Then, walking so softly that we couldn't hear his footsteps, Lew Wasserman exited his door and passed within inches of the two of us without a smile, a nod, or a sound. Why would he acknowledge us? We probably *wanted* something.

More waiting. Then Chudnow couldn't take it. He rushed to the exit door to the staircase, opened it, stepped out, and shut it behind himself. A second later I heard a distant scream, "AHHHHHH!!!!" I cracked up with laughter. All the secretaries looked up at me and frowned except one, Ned Tanen's secretary/assistant, Peggy. She laughed, too.

We met with Tanen, a funny guy, complimentary and accessible. He looked forward to meeting again when we were ready to pitch a movie. Chudnow and I came up with an idea: *Citywars*, about a slightly-distant-future war between two giant city-states, each half of the country, Eastland and Westland. The war was over the last remaining natural resources in the Wyoming town of Chugwater. It was a parody of every classic war movie. All the heroes, the villains, and the weaponry were based upon the differences between stereotyped Southern Californians and New Yorkers.

We designed and printed a newspaper that included headlines, articles, and photographs excerpting the comedy sketches in our movie pitch. Then we phoned Peggy. She was funny and enjoyed our kidding, and we told her our idea: "Chudnow is going to dress like a period newsboy, with a snapped-brim cap and knickers, and deliver the newspaper to Ned Tanen."

"Worst thing you could do," she admonished. "Great idea somewhere else. You remember this office. Ned would be so embarrassed, it would sink like a bomb." I thought, *this is the place that does comedies?!*

* * * *

I directed six pilot episodes of a VH1 TV series called *Shoot the Band*, which was patterned on the popular cable show *Mystery Science Theater 3000*. The series starred four stand-up comics who play in an over-the-hill garage band that hasn't had a gig in thirteen years. They make random phone calls to try to get bookings. Their pitches were "We love Polish hot dogs," to anyone in the phone book with a polish name; "Our grandparents are devout Jews," to names like Steinberg and Weinstein; "We lived in Livorno for two wonderful years," to names like Farino and Gagastino.

The four comics were Mark Cohen, now in Las Vegas playing the role of Joey Bishop in a retro Rat Pack show; Jon Manfrellotti, who did guest shots on *Everybody Loves Raymond*; Craig Anton, who was on *MADtv*; and Walli Cole. Guest stars and writers included Louis Szekely (a.k.a. Louis C.K.), who won an Emmy for his hit TV show, and Dave Attell, who has had several shows on Comedy Central and Martin Olson, who is head writer on the cartoon hit, *Fineas and Ferb.*

The show was shot in New York. I wanted to see what the inside of the stand-up comic world was like. Comedy people know one another, each other's routine, each other's styles. They constantly trade barbs, and they bag on one another to try out jokes.

Remember Gielgud's quote, "Dying is easy. Comedy is hard"? Mark told me, "The owner of the Comedy Cellar held his nose between laughs as a test. If he had to take a breath, that comic never played his place again." The problem was that a new comic would see the owner holding his nose and think the owner was signaling that the comic stunk, so the comic would get so nervous he'd blow the gig one way or the other.

What was The Dream? "To get your own sitcom." The gigs paid twenty-five bucks and a free drink for a set. Sometimes food. At several of the venues, the owner would come to our table and shoot the breeze. They understood the drill. They felt the pain. No one ever complained. The attitude was, "If you can't stand the heat, get outta the fire."

A lot of comics are angry. How do you think they come up with their riffs? Racism, Road rage. Child rearing. Sex. Dating. Bureaucracies. Government. They hate what we all hate. But they vent it in humor: "Wadda you gonna do, shoot yourself? Fahgetabout it, shoot somebody else!"

There was a high. Not just from starting the night with a doob and tossing down drinks backstage. It was pure adrenaline. Win or lose, a packed room with belly laughs coming like bullets in a war zone was as good as it gets. Especially if some agent, or booker, or TV executive caught the show. These guys all wanted to be the next Chris Rock, Dave Chapelle or Jerry Seinfeld.

Like rodeo cowboys, writers, dancers, singers and filmmakers, the chance of a comic's making the dream come true was one in a million. That never held them back. Even in that hypothetical dream room with laughs coming a mile a second, there is *never* an audience in which *everyone* laughs. The smaller the room, the better the chances are that some people will be infected by the laughter around them, though this is not always garunteed. As some comics and cowboys say, “You pays yer money and ya takes yer chances.” Because no six people laugh at the same joke.

Recently, we have seen the passing of two of the most legendary, machine-gun rapid fire, courageous comedians of our generation, Robin Williams and Joan Rivers. They took chances without any second thoughts and I believe they both were incredibly funny from the time they could speak.

And they both knew it.

RULE # 14:

IF YOU DON'T ACT/PERFORM/SCREEN TO A PACKED HOUSE . . . FAHGETABOUT IT!

Before ***KGOD*** was completed, AIP was sold to another studio, Filmways. Filmway's head of production put ***KGOD*** on the shelf. Then Charles Champlin, former critic for the *L.A. Times,* chose it as his entry into the USA film festival, a critics-only festival. He wrote in the *Times:*

> My pick this time was Rick Friedberg's spectacularly irreverent *Pray TV*, co-authored by Dick Chudnow, one of the original Kentucky Fried Theatre group. An outrageous satire on televised religion, it reminds you of Mort Sahl's line, "Are there any groups I haven't offended?" It leaves no pitch unscratched, and the festival audiences on the Southern Methodist University campus cheered it.

KGOD was a major hit at the festival. Therefore, Filmways decided to test market it by screening it to a paying audience in Columbia, Missouri, heart of the Bible Belt, on Easter weekend. This was my Sparta. As Frank Sinatra put it in song, "If you can make it here, you can make it anywhere."

I thought, *Here I go, winging my way to a place most popular with fans of religious right-winger Jerry Falwell, in a section of the country filled with creationists who are pro God, pro guns, anti gays, and anti abortion. And I'm trying to promote a movie that knocks everything about religion.*

I was sent down to do radio and print interviews to hype the film. No money was spent on TV commercials, which is the only way to sell a movie. Any other method, like me warning the media and then shaving my head like a Tibetan monk and painting *Pray TV* on my shaved scalp while sitting in the main intersection of town and setting myself on fire, would fall short. Although I think Filmways would have backed *that* idea—especially if I followed through with the fire part.

No movie gains a potential audience without TV commericals and, also now, advertising on the Internet. Filmways just wanted to see if *anyone* would go see this film, without them spending any money.

A lesson to be learned: If you don't open your movie to a packed house, it will end up in the toilet. That's why you see a barrage of TV commercials for new movies before they come out—they *have* to open.

One solution would have been to kidnap the head of Filmways distribution, throw him in a rat-infested hole, and waterboard him until he agreed to spend money on TV commercials. But I hadn't heard about waterboarding then. The up side was that Columbia is a college town. I did radio interviews with the top local rock-and-roll stations. I figured that youths who listen to rock and roll exercise their freedom of expression from the religious right.

Irony of ironies, the film sold out. The audiences loved it. Here's what the campus reviewer wrote:

> "Friedberg is a young director with a great deal of talent. His sense of cluttered composition recalls early Von Sternberg. Such masterful marshalling of the visual field is more Italianate than American. Several sequences have the garish surrealism of a Fellina Roma and the grotesquerie of stylized homosexual and overweight cameraman

> give the film the air of a working class Satyricon.
>
> In one sequence a born-again black lifer comes on the PTP show by knifing his way through the curtain. He promptly sits down to plug his new book, *Ax Me About God*, with the author, ax in hand, on the cover.
>
> In a spoof of Smokey Robinson and the Village People (WASP cops dance behind the lifer), the murderer sings an amazingly vile song telling how he raped a girl scout because "I didn't like the way her cookies taste."
>
> This is a vulgar classic moment of black comedy, a kind of apotheosis of American Schlock and it stamps Friedberg as no mere hack."
>
> by David Soren, Digest Reviewer

Pretentious as this review might read, I knew I had a potential hit film for college students.

Filmways sold out to Orion Pictures, headed by an infamous former super-agent. He was the quintessential star fucker, wouldn't even *look* at ***KGOD***. He had more lofty ideas. He ran the studio into the ground by commissioning big "star" vehicles with huge budgets Orion didn't have. I think Orion gave him twenty-four hours to get out of town. *I* would have.

Donna Gigliotti, who later produced two of my favorite comedies of all time, ***Shakespeare in Love*** and ***Silver Linings Playbook***, was head of acquisitions for United Artists. She saw ***KGOD*** and tried to buy it for United Artists. But Orion wouldn't sell it. Then she called me up a year later. Now she was head of acquisitions for Orion.

She was bubbling with enthusiasm and said, "I think we can finally buy your film." I laughed and reminded her, "Donna, you *own* it."

Because they were cash poor, Orion sold their entire film library, including ***KGOD,*** which at this point they had retitled ***Pray TV***, to HBO and MGM/UA Video. I called Jim Griffiths, then head of acquisitions at HBO, and asked him, "How's my film doing?" He said,

"So far, it's the best reviewed, most watched film of late night."

"Then why don't you play it in prime time?" I asked.

He laughed and said, "You kidding? A film that knocks religion?!"

HBO was not yet the groundbreaking sophisticated network it became. Later, I ran across a blurb on the Internet entitled "*A Little Gem Before its Time*." Here's the review:

> *"Pray TV* is a dark little comedy about religious broadcasting. It is as biting as it could be for its time when you keep in mind *Pray TV* was made before the various scandals that hit television preachers with the likes of Jim and Tammy Faye Bakker and Jimmy Swaggart.
>
> In a very *Amazon Women On The Moon*–style, *Pray TV* is a series of comedy sketches and funny scenes tied in together with the idea all of this is taking place at television station KGOD after huckster Marvin Fleece, Dabney Coleman, changes the format of 300-watt KRUD out of San Poquito. The staff at family-run KRUD, featuring a newscaster and his ventriloquist's dummy weatherman, the children's show chef Marcia Wallace who does a cooking show in

> español with mucho difficulty-o, the weird exercise show duo featuring a chain-smoking Pee Wee Herman, does its best to follow the new format while Fletcher, the son of the station owner, has a budding romance with an intern.
>
> The sketches in *Pray TV* are very funny and often very surreal. One of the taglines for this movie is "If you don't have a sense of humor, you don't have a prayer," and this is quite true. The auditions for the new KGOD format are hilarious and include a torch singer, who sings about getting on her knees for the Man upstairs, while the programming includes a soap opera titled *One Life To Lose* about Mary trying to hide the identity of her son's father from Joseph. Particularly successful is the PTP Club, which is a great spoof of *The Tonight Show*.
>
> *Pray TV* is a fun little movie, definitely worth watching."

Determined to circumvent Orion, I had a series of screenings for other studios to have them buy and distribute the film. I learned so much about the pain of screening comedies from reading Ralph Rosenblum's book *When the Shooting Stops,* about his years editing for Woody Allen. According to the book, Allen was inconsolable after seeing his first film, alone or with only Rosenblum, way too many times, but Woody's manager told him to phone Mel Brooks who advised,"Go out on the street and find real people to see your movie."

Rosemblum and Allen went to a theater in Greenwich Village and pulled people in off the street to screen the film. And the laughs were there. The moral of the story: "Show the film to people who you think would pay to see it."

Something else, unique to comedies, I learned is what kind of theater is most conducive to comedy screenings—not narrow and deep but wide and shallow, so that the screen envelops the audience; not too air-conditioned and not too warm—nothing to distract people from their comfort zone so they can laugh.

Sherry Lansing, former and first female president of Twentieth Century Fox, had heard about the film. She was a great fan of Dabney Coleman after her hit, ***Nine to Five***. She called me up: "We heard about ***KGOD*** and want to see it. Can you send a print over?"

I was extremely flattered that the head of a studio called me personally, but I said, "Gosh, Sherry, thanks so much for your interest, but I can't do that. I want you to laugh and like it. The last thing I want is a handful of people in a huge theater seeing a broad comedy. I'd be glad to arrange a screening for you anytime that's convenient somewhere off your lot, with some civilians filling the seats and as many people as you want to bring with you." She thanked me and hung up. I knew I blew a potential opportunity but, better to live by your gut feelings than have people see your work in the worst possible light.

The theater must be packed. That's how I chose to screen in a small theater, mostly filled with civilians—people who go to comedy movies to laugh: my kids' friends' parents, neighbors, and friends of friends, leaving only a few middle seats—the best seats—for the VIP movie people who I wanted to buy the film, so they would be surrounded by laughter.

My greatest compliment from these screenings came from Ray Bradbury. He was a lifelong friend of Dick Chudnow's ex-in-laws. He wrote me a note the following day. I've since lost it, but I remember that he loved the film and said it was hilarious—this from one of the most lauded authors in American fiction who had a great sense of humor.

Paul Bluhdorn attended one of these screenings. He was the son of Charles Bluhdorn, former CEO of Gulf and Western, the parent company of Paramount Studios. Paul was head of new acquisitions and recommended ***KGOD*** to Paramount. Paramount passed. The feedback, via Paul, from former studio head Frank Mancuso, was that Frank loved the film, but his sales people were leery about religion.

After a half dozen screenings and feedback via my lawyer from Orion and HBO, I learned that, because it was pre-sold to cable TV, ***KGOD*** was damaged goods. Another one down the drain for me, but an invaluable lesson learned.

Never screen or have your movie screened to an empty house. It's just too intimidating an environment, even to those few that laugh. They look at their neighbors and inhibit themselves from guffawing, lest they come off as low-brow buffoons. I'm sure it's no different for stand-up comics or auditioning actors.

Performing, pitching and, especially showing your work, playing to an empty room is death. Never do it.

If you are interested in seeing a dvd of the movie KGOD/aka Pray TV, it is on dvd on Amazon.

A link to see a short promo is on YouTube at:

http://www.youtube.com/watchv=ewhUY-MfyCU

RULE # 15:

HUMILITY IS A HIGHLY OVERRATED VIRTUE

Fans of movie and television celebrities, artists, comics, writers and singers would like to believe that their favorite artist is someone down to earth—someone a fan could share a joke, a story or a drink with. These same fans forget that their hero or heroine, when seen on talk shows and interviewed in print, are there to sell themselves and their product. If an artist, of any kind, is really talented and has confidence and conviction, my experience is that not *everyone* is humble.

I was used to mixing TV commercial sound tracks with Buzz Knudsen, head sound mixer at Todd AO, who mixed all of Spielberg's movies, winning an academy award for ***E.T.*** and William Friedkin's ***The Exorcist***. He re-mixed ***KGOD*** as a favor because the facility that originally mixed it purposely screwed it up. They were born-again Christians and hated it.

Buzz was outspoken about his feelings about his sound mixing, regardless of how renowned the movie's director was. Between mixing reels of ***Heaven's Gate***, Buzz worked on my film for free. By the way, the ice-skating scene in that movie is one of most stunning scenes I've ever seen on film. It's spine-tingling beautiful. Buzz was a perfectionist and he was uncompromising. Directors like Spielberg and Friedkin, control freaks themselves, relied on Buzz's ears because they, and he, knew he was the best, especially when it came to hearing the dialogue clearly. But in terms of *that*, he was nothing like Richard Portman.

* * * *

After finishing the Standard Oil ad campaign, I agreed to mix the soundtracks at the new Goldwyn Sound Studio in Hollywood. They wanted to attract TV commercial business, and our commercial would be the first.

Goldwyn studios had mixed ***The Gofather*** with Richard Portman, with whom I had also worked. He was Robert Altman's sound mixer, had mixed ***Nashville***, and had won an academy award for ***The Deer Hunter***.

I loved Richard's work. I knew he smoked a lotta dope. I also knew he didn't listen to anyone he didn't respect. I later directed a movie for Frank Mancuso Jr. who phoned his idol, the producer of ***The Godfather***, to get a reference on Portman. This producer told Frank, "Portman's really talented. But he told me to shut up and leave him alone!"

We mixed the commercials in a huge sound-mixing studio. The screen was as large as a movie theater. The speakers were as fine as any music studio. In one commercial, the on-camera Standard Oil spokesman was in Alaska, shouting into his hand-held microphone. You could see his breath because of the cold. Behind him, two giant geodesic tampers were testing the ice for oil. It was visceral, but you didn't hear every syllable perfectly.

Portman, who sported a long ponytail, and I sat at the gigantic mixing board. A dozen guys in suits from BBDO *and* Standard Oil hemmed and hawed. In the sound mix, they asked me to ask Richard if he could make one particular word cut through more clearly. Portman, in his inimitable fashion, turned around in his chair and said, "What the fuck does it matter? It's just a commercial. Nobody watches this shit anyway!"

Ain't much you can say to that. I couldn't anyway. The damage was done. I don't necessarily think the agency suits thought ill of me, but as far as Portman went, I imagine they thought him the devil incarnate. But I know that he believed he was the best in the business. Humility never entered his mind.

* * * *

There are lots of people that excel at their craft in Hollywood. The Academy Awards recognize the finest actors, writers and directors. The Grammy's reward the best singers and songwriters. The Emmy awards bring accolades to creators and performers in television. The Writers Guild and the Directors Guild both accord the finest writer or director of each year. And there are other guilds which recognize the costume designers, production designers, cinematographers, and others.

Performers and technicians who know that they are the best will stand by what they create. Another person I consider to be incredible at his craft was Tim McIntire. Son of John McIntire, star of *Wagon Train*, and Jeannette MacDonald, star of *Gunsmoke*, Tim McIntire was also an actor. He played Alan Freed in ***American Hot Wax*** and the warden in ***Brubaker***.

He was also the hottest voice-over talent in Hollywood—his Orson Wells baritone was recognizable on hundreds of movie trailers and TV commercials. He sometimes did three or four voice-overs in a day. But he hated it. He only wanted to be a singer/songwriter, financing and making his own demos. Tim could play the hell out of any stringed instrument. Jerry Reed, known for his banjo virtuosity, gave Tim a banjo and a couple of lessons. He told me, "Within a year, Tim was as good as anyone I know."

When I finished my documentary on rodeo cowboys, I called Tim, whom I had met when he did voice-overs for some commercials I cut. He told me to bring the film by.

He lived in Beverly Glen canyon with his actress wife, Kelly Jean Peters, the female lead opposite Robert Redford in ***The Great Waldo Pepper***.

Tim offered to score my entire film and already had a theme song in mind for the opening credits. I was so grateful I didn't know what to say. For the title song, we went into a studio in Hollywood with a twenty-four-track board. Tim was a big guy, constantly fighting his weight. Lined up on the narrow shelf in front of the mixing board was a smorgasbord of fortification: a jelly jar of cocaine, a half-dozen joints, a bottle of Southern Comfort, beer, potato chips, and cookies. I doubt this was the number-one diet on AA or Weight Watchers.

First he played through the theme song he'd written for me, "*Ride in the Rodeo*," about a crippled kid who couldn't walk. In the song, the kid's parents tied him onto a horse, and he became a bronc rider. Genius. It captured the essence of cowboy macho and touched your heart at the same time.

Tim had already laid the tracks and was ready to mix them. I sat in awe as he snorted a line of coke, took a toke of weed and a sip of booze, and adjusted whatever equalizer knob he thought appropriate. Here's some of Tim's lyrics from "Ride in the Rodeo":

Well Mary had a baby but she didn't call him Jesus.
She called him Billy Bob after Papa Buttrey's dad.

Now Billy only had one good foot,
the other one looked like a pine tree root.
So it seemed like all the Buttrey's luck was bad.

There was a doctor in Cheyenne, said do everything you can to make him feel like every other child.

So they took Billy Bob to the Cheyenne Fair

and Billy saw somethin' while he was there
that drove him plumb stark mad dog ravin' wild.

He saw that whole big show and he knew just
where he wanted to go and he whooped and he
hollered and he told his mama so.

Said, Mama, I wanna ride, ride, ride,
I wanna ride in the rodeo,
I wanna ride in the Big Time rodeo . . .

The film won every film festival it entered: Atlanta, Dallas, San Francisco, and the coveted Cine Golden Eagle. I sold four hundred copies to the USIA to play in their offices around the world. It was then picked up by Doubleday Publishing's film department, which sold hundreds of copies to schools. It was reviewed by an educational film reviewer, who wrote:

> "The excitement, thrills, spills, and special color of rodeo are well known to the spectator; however, this film is an intimate look at those men who make a living from riding in rodeos and, in essence, provides a portrait of the classic American folk hero—the cowboy.
>
> Most of the action was filmed at the world's oldest and largest rodeo, Cheyenne Frontier Days. But the focus remains on the men themselves, and through interviews and voice-overs, the dreams of greatness, the disappointments, and the physical hurt begin to betray themselves. It is the camaraderie and the dependence of friend upon friend and man upon animal which predominates and which presents a new view of the men who follow this sport. "
>
> Recommended. Landers Film Reviews

Sadly, over the next few years, I lost track of Tim. I heard he'd been fired and blackballed in the voice-over world for missing recording sessions or fucking them up. And I was informed that he had become the voice of Honda Motorcycles.

They gave him a Honda Ninja, a monster of a bike. He crashed it and broke his back. Split from Kelly who couldn't stand by and see him self-destruct, he got hooked on pain pills and when he was only forty, he flipped his bike and killed himself. The world lost one of the most talented artists I'd ever known to drugs, self-destruction, and rock and roll—all of which are not mutually exclusive.

There's a lotta pain in "doing your own thing." So many artists, writers, performers, and other creative forces have resorted to drugs and alcohol for reasons stemming from calming the demons within to insecurity over their abilities to a superstitious dependency upon an artificial motivator. But we can't judge these artists for their addictions. We also can't ever discover if these addictions were the cause of great work.

Buzz Knudsen, Richard Portman, George Clayton Johnson and Tim McIntire were all respected for doing great work. That work is what will survive, not the memories of the lack of humility they displayed.

One sees interviews on *Entertainmen Tonight* and the various talk shows with movie and TV stars, comics, musicians, prominent writers, directors and producers. These interviews are set up by highly paid publicists and the interviewees are coached to come off media friendly. The purpose of the interview is for the interviewee to sell their book, their concert or their movie to the largest audience possible by seeming to be humble and down to earth--the kind of person America will like and want to see. But the work that person 'plugs' is what will make these potential ticket buyers into bonafide fans.

RULE # 16:

IT DOESN'T MATTER WHAT THEY SAY ABOUT YOU AS LONG AS THEY SPELL YOUR NAME CORRECTLY

I have the dubious distinction of having directed four of the five music videos that Al Gore's ex-wife,Tipper Gore, used to demonstrate to Congress the need to establish the PMRC (Parents' Music Resource Center), a group to censor "inappropriate" music by putting a "contains explicit lyrics or content" disclaimer on CDs and downloads.

The videos were Van Halen's "Hot for Teacher," W.A.S.P's "Blind in Texas" and "Wild Child," and Y & T's "Summertime Girls." I turned down the invitation to direct the fifth video on Tipper's list: "Smokin' in the Boys' Room" by Mötley Crüe. (Nikki Sixx called me and asked if I wanted to direct the video, but I was set to direct an episode of the prime-time return of *The Twilight Zone* to TV.) I was chosen to direct these videos because hard rock and heavy metal groups had a difficult time getting airplay from MTV. Their videos were sexist and violent. Mine were story driven and funny.

I had a lot of autonomy and fun creating and directing music videos. W.A.S.P is the hair band in the movie ***This Is Spinal Tap***. I pitched them a concept: "What if we take you guys . . ." they ranged from six foot four to six foot six " . . . into the old Wild West and no one cares?" They liked it. We went to the Western movie set in Old Tucson. We filmed the group coming into town like hired gunslingers, entering the vintage saloon where mean hombres shot six-shooters in the air as W.A.S.P performed "Blind in Texas."

The video endears the band to the tough cowboys when Blackie Lawless, lead singer, opens his guitar case and lifts out his pet armadillo. Painted black with NASCAR logos affixed to its tough skin, Blackie's rodent wins the armadillo race.

I set up a classic Western Movie shot atop a two-story building, with a cowboy's gun belt and the railing in the foreground, shooting down the Western street into the sun so that the morning sunrise would backlight the group coming into town. It would be cool, macho, cinematic. The sun was rising, we had ten minutes left, and we still had no band. Then, directly at the end of the dirt street, appeared the four guys in black leather—the bassist, Chris, wore chrome baseball catcher's shin guards—and they sauntered toward the camera like bad asses from hell. Money!

The female lead would be Rosa, as in Marty Robbins's classic "El Paso": *"Out in the West Texas town of El Paso, I fell in love with a Mexican girl."* But Rosa needed to be cast. We asked the college girls working in the bars and restaurants in Tucson, "Do you know a knock-out Latina girl who would like to be in a music video?" They all came up with the same idea: Their college mate who just won the Miss New Mexico contest. A waitress phoned her. She showed up with her two brothers. She was statuesque and gorgeous. The band was gentlemanly. Her brothers agreed to allow her to be in the video. Every male on the crew hit on her. No luck.

After the shoot, we all went out to celebrate. Blackie begged off, saying, "I got a headache like a vise grip," and returned to the motel. He said, "I'm really sick, man. You guys go on ahead. I'll see you in L.A."

A week later, back in L.A., there was Blackie with Miss New Mexico. He told us, "I just got back from Mexico. Had to meet the parents, guarantee my honorable intentions." He took her hand and displayed a diamond the size of a malt ball. I wish I had a snapshot of her parents' faces when they met Blackie.

Years later, I was a guest lecturer at a class of graduate film students at UCLA. A young filmmaker from Japan showed me a Japanese music magazine that listed my videos as the top four in the top one hundred heavy metal videos of all time. Yeah me, dubious distinction notwithstanding.

"Dude," a publicist once told me, "take ink wherever you can get it." He was right. I got phone calls from people who heard about the videos.

* * * *

Susan Zwerman, one of the top visual effects producers (***The last Jedi and Black Panther***) called. She asked if I was interested in doing a 3-D video based upon a song Edgar Winter had written for L. Ron Hubbard, founder and head of Scientology. "It's an anti-drug science-fiction story," she explained. I asked her, "Scientology . . . I don't know . . . aren't they like a cult?" She assured me, "Don't worry, we're not selling Scientology. This is going to be premiered on MTV on a Saturday night, using new 3-D TV technology."

"Wow," I exclaimed, "3-D, that's awesome!" She replied, "Yeah, and to go along with that, Rhino Records are going to advertise it on radio to hype the music audiences."

Susan had worked as a line producer, and production manager and knew how to budget and make things happen. She said, "I'll set a meeting up with the Scientology and Rhino Records people." "Color me there," I told her.

We went to the Scientology building on Hollywood Boulevard, a block from Grauman's Chinese Theatre. We were ushered into a large conference room and sat perpendicular to four Scientology executives, who were all dressed in dark suits, white shirts and muted ties.

Directly across from us were the two owners of Rhino Records, bearded guys in Hawaiian shirts who smelled like marijuana. The Scientology guys looked at the Rhino guys like they were fungi under a microscope.

I pitched the video to everyone. The Scientology guys loved it. The Rhino Records guys were too cool for school. They may have liked it, but they wouldn't show it. I soon found out why. "How much is this going to cost?" they asked. Susan handed them copies of the budget and said, "Two hundred and fifty thousand dollars."

The Scientology guys didn't flinch. The Rhino Records guys went ballistic and huffed,"What?!!" Susan took it in stride. She told them, "It's all shot in one set. I know top people who will kill to make the props, wardrobe, and set decorations, but, because it's 3-D, we have to shoot two cameras locked together and more lights than normal. For a video like this, it's extremely inexpensive."

The Rhino guys were outraged. These guys believed in buying for a nickel and selling for ten bucks. We shook hands all around, knowing that, if the Scientology people were the only ones involved, we'd have made that video. I have no regrets. I'd have loved directing that video, especially after ***Avatar*** set the 3-D trend that became so prevalent in big-budget studio spectacles like ***Life of Pi, Rise of the Planet of the Apes, Guardians of the Galaxy,*** etc, etc.. However, I know more now than I did then about Scientology. I'm glad I didn't help them sell their pseudo-religious nuttery.

With each music video I did make, there was lots of press. The videos are made to sell CDs and downloads on iTunes. Even before YouTube, the record company wanted as much publicity as they could get. Despite some parents who were concerned over their kid's choice of music (not a new phenomenon), music video makers attempt to appeal to these kids with funny and/or outrageous videos. Since I fell into that category, I got a lot of ink. Which, I imagine, resulted in more work. Thereby proving, at least to me, that I really doesn't matter what they say about you (unless there's clear evidence you're an ax murderer), as long as your name is mentioned in the entertainment press.

If you are interested in seeing the W.A.S.P. music video, "*Blind in Texas*," you can find it on You Tube at:

https://www.youtube.com/watch/v=4fDKisklzQI

RULE # 17:

BE WARY OF TRYING ANYTHING NEVER DONE BEFORE . . . THEN TRY IT ANYWAY

From the In the *Line of Fire* parody scene

Most every difficult or tricky movie shot has been planned and/or done by at least one or several of the crew on a studio movie. But each new trick requires something never *exactly* done before. The photo above is a perfect example of this.

The opening scene in ***Spy Hard*** is a spoof of ***In the Line of Fire***. Leslie Nielsen's character, Dick Steele, Agent WD-40, like Clint Eastwood's character in ***In the Line of Fire***, is an over-the-hill secret service agent. He thinks he hears a gunshot, even though it's only a kid popping a balloon. He immediately throws the President of the United States into the presidential limousine, bashing the poor guy's head in the process.

Then, to ensure the president's safety, Leslie starts to chase the president's limo on foot. The limo approaches a tollbooth at the base of a draw bridge and smashes through the red and white diagonally-striped barrier arm. Leslie, still running, approaches the same tollbooth and smashes through a much smaller red and white diagonally-striped barrier arm meant for pedestrians.

The limo speeds onto the bridge. Leslie, trying to catch up to the limo, reacts to a squawk in his headset as he hears, "Stop! The bridge is up!" The limo passes a warning barrier, comprised of flashing lights and those orange cylinders you see on street repair sites. The limo slams on the brakes, goes into a skid, does a 180-degree turn, and ends up with its back half hanging over the edge of the open draw bridge, fifty feet above water.

Leslie, his shoes leaving sole tracks (like the tire skid tracks from the limo), also screeches to a halt, also does a 180, and ends up with his heels hanging over the bridge's edge, also fifty feet above the water. The limo and Leslie teeter. We hear the creaking of the car and of Leslie's shoes. Leslie slowly and gingerly reaches into his back pocket and pulls out his fat wallet. He transfers it to his chest pocket, shifting the extra weight, and rights himself, out of danger.

He immediately rushes to the front of the limo, pulls out the special cable embedded in his spy wristwatch, and ties it around the front bumper of the limo. Reeling out the cable as he backs up, he ties the cable to an orange plastic safety cone in the construction barrier. Removing his wristwatch, he slips it over the top of the cone, pulling the cable taut.

Just then comes another squawk on Leslie's headset and he hears, "Steele, Rancor [the bad guy] has been located! Repeat, Rancor has been located. We're coming to pick you up."

Police cars, with lights flashing and sirens blaring, speed to the rescue. A chopper swoops in and lands. Leslie hops in the chopper, flashing a thumbs-up to the president's limo. As they're lifting off, Leslie feels something in his shirt pocket. He pulls out a piece of red-and-white-striped barrier he had broken through at the tollgate. He thinks nothing of it and tosses it out the chopper's open door.

In a parody of the slow motion falling leaf that opens ***Forrest Gump***, the chip falls ever so slowly down and lands softly on the trunk lid of the limo, still teetering on the bridge. Just like the pigeon that landed on the bad guys' stolen truck in ***True Lies***, this is the final straw. Ludicrously, the extra weight makes the difference. The limo starts to fall, carrying the cable and plastic construction cone with it, and plummets into the drink.

Our location was a drawbridge in San Pedro. We built a faux set of tollbooths at the base of the bridge. We shot all the necessary scenes up to the point of the limo drop. We had cameras covering the limo, the bridge, and a remotely-operated technocrane extended out over the bridge's lip, and another remote camera that would photograph from atop the bridge. The limo was held by a cable hidden beneath a humongous steel plate laid atop the bridge's tarmac—something that had never been done before.

We were below, on a deck built into the water, to film the action above. The final shot would be the limo falling as the helicopter flies by with Leslie's double inside the open doorway. We wanted to film the chopper flying directly across the setting sun, just as the limo fell. Movie magic. A lotta thought. A lotta work. One take. That's all we'd get. The Weather Service told us what time the sun would set. The chopper had to replace its door and fly back to Van Nuys during daylight. That gave us maybe a ten-minute window when the sun was low enough to include in the shot and before the chopper had to leave.

We set up all eight cameras in order to be ready to shoot at 6:00 PM. Then we got a call from the Port Authority. "There's a boat coming through in fifteen minutes," the guy said. We had to telescope the technocrane back and raise the bridge to its full height. This was like running a full-scale, four-alarm fire drill in the middle of Manhattan in the middle of the night in the middle of summer. We moved in triple speed to do it. The boat came through. We scurried to replace everything. We were set again.

Director of Photography John Leonetti (***The Mask, Hot Shots! Part Deux*** and ***The Conjuring*** and now director ***of Annabelle***), usually a positive guy, put his arm around my shoulders and said, "I'm sorry boss, but we gotta change film stock. If we don't use high-speed film, the water will be black, and the limousine's already black, and you won't see a damned thing when it goes in the drink." I admonished him in my best *Godfather* voice, "Okay, John, but if we don't get the shot, you'll be sleepin' wid da limo," and I told him to proceed.

We were set to go at 6:05. Forty of us were on a deck, on the water, below the bridge, looking up at the limo hanging over. I had a remote monitor that showed what the technocrane would see as the chopper flew by the sunset and the limo was cut loose and fell.

I asked the assistant director and chopper pilot on walkie-talkie, "Is there enough time for one rehearsal fly-by for camera?" The pilot replied, "No, but let's do it anyway." On cue, he flew the chopper by, in the background. It was too high to cover the sun. I told him to adjust.

We were already ten minutes late. We had to go. You could've heard a pin drop. The A.D. called, "Roll cameras!" and each camera reported in: "Camera one rolling"; "Camera two rolling"; etc. I called, "Action!" and the chopper began its approach. The special effects guy released the cable holding the limo. And I watched as the chopper flew by the sun just as the limo dropped. I smiled from ear to ear. The limo plummeted into the water. The splash shot thirty feet into the air. Everyone applauded and cheered. It was incredible!!!

Elements of this stunt had been done before. But the specific rigs and devices we built were never before used. We were proud that everything came off as planned and was spectacular. Disney, after previews, cut the scene to smithereens. It didn't have what they love best about cartoon comedies—someone, in close up, hit over the head with a frying pan. But we did something not exactly done before because everyone involved believed we could.

If you're interested in seeing ***Spy Hard***, you can find it on dvd on Amazon.com or stream it on Amazon Prime and if you want to see the original trailer for it, you can find an HD version on Vimeo at:

https://vimeo.com/49515890

RULE # 18:

NEVER WORK WITH KIDS OR ANIMALS. REALIZE *THEY'RE* IN CHARGE . . . *YOU'RE* NOT

The CityKids Foundation is a group of multi-cultural youths that sing, dance, act, and compose music while learning how to get along with one another. They had just joined the Jim Henson Company to produce a television series to be broadcast on ABC TV. With great stories and music videos, this was a ground-breaking childrens's show . . . the forerunner to the long-running TV hit, *Glee*.

I met with Brian Henson, Alex Rockwell, and Ritamarie Peruggi, executive producers of the show who were more passionate about their work than the attendant bullshit that goes with network TV series—like money, which, in this case, wasn't abundant. They hired me to direct the first three shows of twelve. I moved to New York, and I was forewarned, "You are going to fall in love with Adriana Trigiani." That was an understatement.

Adriana Trigiani was the show runner—executive producer/head writer; youth wrangler; and diplomat par excellence. She had been a writer/producer on *The Bill Cosby Show* and its spin-off, *A Different World.* Adri had many opportunities to move to Hollywood and make it big in television—not her thing. Television writers in Hollywood are less concerned with what's on the page than how big and where their name is in the credits. She went on to become a *New York Times* bestselling novelist with her *Big Stone Gap* trilogy and a dozen succeeding novels, including an incredible epic love story about her grandparents called *The Shoemaker's Wife.* In addition, she has written and directed a movie, ***Big Stone Gap***, based upon her first novel.

Adriana is a large woman from a larger Italian family with family values, morals,and ethics. She encouraged and mentored youths from the CityKids foundation to contribute to scripts and music for the series.

The TV series was about seven high school seniors, two African-American, two Puerto Rican, one Asian, one Jewish, and one white Protestant. It dealt with the gut issues of the day: dating, work, sex, cliques, friendships, loyalty, honesty, competition, and so on. Although the story lines were funny, they were substantive and relevant.

The pace and style of the show was heightened by music videos that exemplified the story line. An extra attraction for me were the short snippets of Muppets—two high school girl puppets acting as a classical Greek chorus that criticized the storyline and the characters.

Shooting muppets was a trip. Dabney Coleman, who starred in the second Muppet's movie, ***The Muppets Take Manhattan***, warned me that, at some point, I would be anthropomorphizing puppets: "I was standing by a set, and Kermit the frog came up behind me and struck up a conversation. I spoke to him just like I'm speaking to you!"

Several of the crew grumbled about how unruly some of the young actors were, but for many of the kids, this was their first job. The crew didn't realize how incredibly talented these kids were. Dulé Hill, Lisa Marie Carson, Dash Mihok, Donald Faison, Renoly Santiago, and Malik Yoba would go on to fame in network TV and movies. I've seen other members of that cast doing guest shots on TV series and TV commercials. *I* knew how good they were.

It was a grueling experience for these kids, some of whom were still in school, all of whom came from lower-or working-class families, and all of them worked long hours rehearsing dialogue, dance steps, and music lyrics. A few were sometimes late to work. Others sometimes were tired and got cranky. But all of them put their all into their work.

After directing the first episode, the company asked me to do the second set of three shows (the production was geared to one director doing three episodes as a second director prepped the next three). During the second set, I directed an episode written entirely by Adriana. I thought it was the best and funniest of all twelve episodes. The writing was terrific; the adult actors, who were all friends of Adriana, were funny; the music lyrics for the videos about ecology were relevant; and the Muppets' comments were hilarious. Watching Adri in action, endearing herself to the parents of the cast who were working such long and arduous hours, was amazing. This woman could run a country.

Fortunately by that time I was a father of three, a baseball coach of dozens, and a mentor to my kids' friends. What I quickly learned from these experiences is that all kids are different and have to be treated as such. One can't come on like Attila the Hun nor the Flying Nun. Kids need to be recognized as individuals.

One more thing—because this chapter includes animals. Animals also have to be treated as individuals. Don't talk down to them. But never forget, you're the alpha and they need to be the zeta. If you treat them as equals, they'll demand more lines and close ups. If you think they don't care about stardom, you're wrong. As far as animals are concerned, they don't speak English, but, although they respond to praise and punishment, just like people, they'd really rather eat than act. Matter of fact, the treatment you use to praise animals—rewarding them with a treat—may not be a bad idea for kids and adult actors. So keep some paté in your pocket for human stars and tell them something along the lines of, "Good job, Angelina. Good girl!"

RULE # 19:

IN SHOW BIZ, A FRIEND IN NEED IS A FRIEND INDEED . . . AS LONG AS YOU KEEP FULFILLING THEIR NEEDS

Where I grew up, in Cheyenne, Wyoming, a friend is usually someone you attended school with and maybe you played sports or studied with them too. The rule of thumb was, without thinking, they had your back no matter what. Such is not always the case in Hollywood, where "friends" are easily and quickly acquired and more easily and rapidly lost in the process of climbing the show biz ladder.

Even though Paramount passed on picking up ***KGOD***, I got a phone call two days later. The man on the line had a New York accent, and got right to the point: "I saw your film and thought it was funny. I have a treatment for a prison comedy, and I want you to direct it," he said. It was Frank Mancuso, Jr. I started to answer, but he cut me off, saying, "Meet me at the Beverly Wilshire tomorrow for breakfast." I said, "Okay," and I phoned my lawyer to ask him to join me.

The next morning, Frank Jr., who I called Frank, handed me a thin treatment called *Off the Wall* by the writer of ***Friday the 13th***, which Frank Jr. produced. He told me, "I want you to direct it." I quickly replied, "Okay."

Frank Jr. and I became friends. He's extremely charming, an incredibly savvy guy with a wicked sense of humor. I found him an apartment near my home. For the next weeks we drove night and day, delivering scripts to the homes of actors like Danny de Vito in the hope we could cast some people we liked for the lead characters.

The film was a copy of ***Stir Crazy***, an old movie the financiers wanted to reproduce. The script was rushed to beat an alleged writer's strike, but I thought we could improve it as we shot—never a good idea. Our two young leads were not comedy guys—making it an even worse idea. I overlooked what every director knows: Good movies start with a good script and good cast. We had neither. We had secondary characters and background jokes by the boatload, but no funny in the foreground where the funny should be.

We shot it entirely on location in South Central L.A. at an abandoned Goodyear Tire factory. It had humongous floors, exposed pillars, and floor-to-ceiling mullioned windows, all built around a central grassy area we'd use for the prison exercise yard.

We built the warden's office in an enclosed bridge that spanned two large factory buildings and overlooked the exercise yard. We filled the yard with off-beat prisoners: weight lifters, hopscotchers, break dancers, transvestites in high heels, and a pair of Siamese twins joined at the arm, who shared a prison-striped shirt.

Paul Sorvino, who was terrific, played the insane warden who hallucinates that he hears aliens in his head. His intern for the summer was played by Dick Chudnow, whose name is Moscowitz. Dick and Paul came up with some hilarious dialogue for themselves. Here's an example:

> WARDEN: Moscowitz, you know what I look for in a man?"

(Chudnow is five foot three. Sorvino is six foot three.)

> MOSCOWITZ (sarcastic): "No,sir, I don't."

WARDEN takes a step closer.

WARDEN: What he says.

WARDEN steps forward, closer to MOSCOWITZ.

WARDEN: What he does.

WARDEN steps up to within inches and looms over MOSCOWITZ.

WARDEN: And how tall he is.

After we finished shooting ***Off the Wall***, Frank Jr. flew my wife and me to New York to meet his parents. We first met Frank Mancuso Sr. and his wife, Faye, at Frankie and Johnny's, a famed steakhouse in Midtown Manhattan. The owner came to our table. Frank Sr. introduced us: "This is Laurel and Rick Friedberg," he said. It was a sign of respect I always notice, especially in Hollywood: when someone calls you by your name. When they don't, you know you're not on their list of people they need to know.

* * * *

Frank Jr. asked me to direct ***Friday the 13th Part 3-D*** for them, but I declined because I thought I was destined for higher profile movies. I knew the biggest obstacle would be the problematic two-camera stereovision 3-D rig that weighed a ton and required a warehouse of lights to bring the light level up to what was required for 3-D filming. I was not a horror film afficionado and I thought I should hold out for a better opportunity.

This was yet another mistake I've made. I should've taken this job because we would've started once we finished ***Off the Wall***. Here's a cardinal rule: Book your next job before you finish your last one. Hollywood insiders only want someone with "heat." Having just directed a movie places you five rungs higher on the flavor-of-the-week ladder.

We finished filming ***Off the Wall***, "locked" picture, and were now ready to score the music. A film scoring session is a thrilling spectacle. Studio musicians are placed in groups based on instrument type: the horns in a horn section, the strings in the string section, and the like. Each group is always deep in conversation. Though I'd like to think they talk about the music cues, they actually talk about their cars, their mortgage rates, their kids' schools, who's boffing whom, and the crappy producers and directors they've worked with.

Off the Wall had a very stylistic scene for which the score had not been composed. In the middle of the studio, set in a U formation, sat the three top Moog synthesizer players of the day: Mike Boddicker, Mike Lang, and Ian Underwood. They'd all played on albums for the Beatles, the Stones, and countless others. Their assignment was to "wing it"—to come up with something out-of-this-world stylistic for the fight scene in ***Off the Wall***, a dream sequence reminiscent of ***Raging Bull***. And they did. Incredible!

Irrespective of this score and the terrific dialogue Sorvino and Chudnow had come up with, ***Off the Wall*** was a forgettable film—it was too rushed and not well cast—and it was not picked up for distribution by Paramount. Frank Sr. recused himself from the process since it was his son's film. Frank Jr. was devastated; it was a personal defeat for him. He didn't speak to me again, until, years later, when he wrote me a personal note wishing me good luck with ***Spy Hard***.

Although it was painful to be totally cut off from Frank, every close friend I'd known for years was not surprised. It was not about Frank. It was about business. Show

Business makes ties that bind, but it can also cut them loose as if they've never existed.

* * * *

My agent, Jane Sindell, later producer of ***Seabiscuit***, started to seek out opportunities for me to direct another film. She set me up with Jennings Lang an old timer who coincidentally was the father of Mike Lang, reknowned synthesizer player on ***Off the Wall***.

Jennings had an office on the Universal Studios lot. He produced ***Airport 1975, Airport '77***, and ***The Concord . . . Airport '79***. But Lang's bigger claim to fame was that, as a young agent, he was caught in bed with a movie star, Joan Bennett. Her producer husband shot Lang in the testicle. The joke was that one could now refer to him as "Jenning" instead of Jennings.

He wanted to produce a military comedy, like ***Stripes***, with Eddie Murphy. "Jenning" was in his seventies and was as tall standing up as sitting down. I sat across from him while, puffing on a fat cigar, he was on the phone with Eddie's New York lawyer, and he shouted, "What the fuck are you talking about, he's a *schvartze*! These *Saturday Night Live* guys are like a fart in a windstorm!" After whatever retort came through, he banged his phone down. He looked at me and said, "The guy wants fifty grand to supervise the script. Who the hell is going to give him that kind of dough?!"

The blood drained from my face. Every star from *Saturday Night Live* had made a blockbuster comedy within the last two years. Eddie Murphy was hilarious. My one shot at the big time was just blown out the window by this one-balled little runt who was quibbling over Universal's money. It wasn't even his money! I remembered a Hollywood aphorism attributed to producers: "Never use your own money." This time it came back to haunt me.

Days later, Hildy Gottlieb, an agent who had the office next to Jane, heard about the exchange with Eddie Murphy's lawyer. She represented Murphy. She also represented the director Walter Hill, who was casting a cop movie. She asked Hill if he had a role for Murphy. Hill had not yet cast Nick Nolte's sidekick and was open to suggestion.

Eddie Murphy was cast. ***48 Hours*** was a megahit. Eddie Murphy was hysterical. His "quote" as an actor went from fifty thousand to a million bucks. But "Jenning" wouldn't spend other people's money on a "*schvartze*."

I lost a shot at climbing another rung of the movie ladder, and I also lost someone I considered a friend. But there are far worse characters in Hollywood, and it's rare to find producers that can laugh and support you—at least until their movies bomb.

Remembering how and when you made friends in school, in sports, in work and play, one sometimes forgets that these ties that bound you were not related to what you did or did not do to secure that friend by furthering their career profile.

RULE # 20:

GETTING A FILM GREEN LIT IS A TEST OF WILL

Making films is difficult. Just like Cheyenne ranchers who have to birth a calf in the middle of a field in the damn wind, or ford a stream with a lame horse, or lash a fence post with baling wire—in the film industry, ya do whacha gotta do. But those Cheyenne metaphors apply to the physical making of films, not the political ones. *Everything* surrounding the making of a film is a test of will.

What I could never be prepared for were the politics of getting a film commissioned. In the industry, we call this getting the "green light." But the process is heart ripping—it has the potential to ruin the joy of it all. It's just like how real politics ruins the joy of running a country, or like Russian judges ruin the joy of competing in the Olympics, or like Sarah Palin taking the joy out of sex, reading, and (to some) geography. Maneuvering the shark-infested waters of Studio Land is as tough as it gets.

I directed Leslie Nielsen in TV commercial campaigns for Dollar Rent A Car that were shown during the Super Bowl, the NBA Playoffs, and the World Series. As an avid golfer, Leslie asked me to direct two home video golf instruction parodies, written by Henry Beard, co-editor of the *Harvard Lampoon* and, later, *National Lampoon.* Henry is enviably smart and funny. He wrote several humorous books on golf, one of which, *Mulligan's Laws*, was filled with hysterical one-liners like: "Does a nonchalant putt count as many strokes as a chalant putt?"

The golf videos were quite successful, and, after success of the commercial campaigns and the videos, I approached Leslie with a script my son, Jason, and his partner wrote in their senior year in college. It was a James Bond spoof. I gave it to Leslie and he agreed to do it, as long as my partner, Dick Chudnow, and I rewrote it for him. He was uncomfortable working with two twenty-year-olds and hinted that he'd like to receive writing credit instead of giving it to Jason and Aaron. I told Leslie that the credits would be up to the Writers Guild. I wanted to ensure Jason and Aaron received a writing credit on a movie that is produced, which is almost essential to getting another job.

My manager took the revised screenplay to a lawyer who will remain unnamed, hopefully for life. This lawyer, unbeknownst to us, was on the way out of the firm he worked for, which was also headed for the toilet. He offered us a minimal amount to option the script and rewrite it. Here it is important to remember that in Hollywood, image is everything; this lawyer had a penthouse office and drove a seven series BMW. So what did I know? He said he could get financing for our script. He could have lived in a refrigerator carton and driven a shopping cart.

The lawyer sent the screenplay to a "dear friend" at New Line Cinema, a smaller but successful Hollywood studio. Managers, agents, and producers all have "dear friends." The term applies to anyone they've ever met or anyone they've wanted to meet but have never had a good enough project to present.

Hollywood studio executives never read screenplays. The execs turn submitted screenplays over to lesser employees for "coverage." Coverage is a two-page synopsis with a summation of whether or not to consider pursuing the screenplay. Our screenplay coverage was made by the head of the "story department," Mark

Ordesky. He loved the script. Here's the final excerpt of his coverage:

> COMMENTS: I still find this very funny, even on the second reading, and definitively say to CONSIDER it. The characters are great, the dialogue is very funny, the spoof is very well done, the plays on modern and not so modern movies is witty, and I think it will be quite commercial, as I've mentioned previously.

Ordesky rose in the New Line ranks. He shepherded the ***Lord of the Rings*** franchise and eventually became Head of Production. His coverage of our screenplay engendered a meeting with his boss, a woman known for "art" films and the "dear friend" of the unnamed lawyer. A good script to her would have a downtrodden character who wears a paper shirt and does lines of coke off the back of endangered species because he may, by doing so, save the world.

The New Line meeting was with me, Mr. Unnamed Lawyer, my manager, Mark Ordesky, and Ms. Art Film Afficionado. She turned to me, knowing Leslie Neilsen was attached to star in our film, and said, "You know, I went to see that film ***The Naked Gun***. The entire audience was laughing. I didn't understand why." She continued, "I'll take a look at the script and let you know."

As New Line's art house executive, she passed on the screenplay. I seriously doubt she read it. A good indication of this was her comment about "looking at the script." That usually means glancing at the cover as it's flung onto the shredding pile.

I called a real friend, Terry Spazek, former head of physical production for Ron Howard and Brian Grazer's company, Imagine Films. He did a budget for our script, and he contacted an acquaintance at Aaron Spelling's company, which was successful in TV with *Charlie's*

Angels and *90210*. This acquaintance was co-head of the movie division along with Denis Pregnolato, for whom I directed a music video.

They liked the script and thought the budget practical. They required Leslie to attend a meeting with me, my manager, and Mr. Unnamed Lawyer who, through his contact with my manager, had become permanently attached as co-producer. (Funny how these things snowball. Leslie was attached because I directed his commercials and golf videos. My son and his partner were of course involved because they wrote the original script. Dick and I re-wrote it, without any help, so we were obviously in. My friend Terry got us to Spelling, so he was in. Yet we now had two producers attached who had done nothing.)

The execs at Spelling said we had a deal subject to Aaron Spelling's approval. We waited weeks for his response. The real reason we couldn't get an answer was because these execs were waiting for the perfect moment to find Aaron in the perfect mood. Finally we received a pass—–it was a total shock.

I called Denis, who I knew to be a straight shooter. He told me Aaron required the approval of Frank Mancuso, who was now head of MGM. MGM owned the James Bond franchise, a notoriously litigious group when it comes to James Bond. Spelling, an ex super agent, refused to make the call. He didn't want to put Mancuso in an uncomfortable position, knowing how difficult it could be to deal with the Broccoli family, who owned the James Bond franchise.

* * * *

My manager next approached Joe Roth, head of production at Disney. Joe spearheaded ***Hot Shots! Part Deux***, and he was known for liking spoofs. Leslie, my manager, the infamous unnamed-lawyer-now-co-producer, and I met with Joe and a young exec, who worked on Disney's biggest hit that previous year, ***The Santa Clause***.

Roth liked the script. He asked Leslie, "You're going to star?" "Yes," Leslie confirmed. Joe turned to me and asked, "You're going to direct?""Yes," I told him. Joe went on, "This is your basic *MAD Magazine* style, right?" "You got it." We parodied every contemporary reference to movies, TV, music videos, and pop culture. He asked us to delete some scenes and to "Make all the parodies male-oriented action movies."

The meeting ended with his summation: "Charles [the young exec], will tell you his thoughts on a rewrite. If we like it, we'll make it." Roth got up and left. We all felt on top of the world and filed out. Charles pulled me aside in the hall and told me, "The first sixty pages are fine. Add some action movie spoofs." I thought to myself, *Yes, sir!*

We were given a month to rewrite. If it was not accepted, we could reclaim the script. We rewrote, deleting some funny scenes and adding spoofs of ***True Lies***, ***Speed***, and ***Cliffhanger***, and turned it over in three weeks. Two days later, we got a green light.

Before pre-production, we met with the heads of the business and legal departments of Disney to discuss the ramifications of buying back the screenplay from the nearly defunct company for which our unnamed lawyer/co-producer had worked.

There were more than a dozen suits sitting around the conference table with my manager, Mr. Unnamed, and me. Among the executives was the physical production executive assigned to our movie, Su Armstrong. She was an Australian who'd been production manager for director Peter Weir (***The Truman Show, Master and Commander, Dead Poets Society***). I'd already had the requisite "lunch" with her—she was skeptical how I could possibly shoot this film in less time and with less money than she believed would be necessary, but she asked knowledgeable questions and she accepted my answers.

During the meeting, Mr. Unnamed pontificated on how much he had developed the script and how important he was in getting Leslie Neilsen on board. One by one, the executives either checked their watches or simply excused themselves and left. Mr. Unnamed was about as popular in this room as a vulture on your sick bed. After the meeting, Su phoned me and advised, "Do yourself a favor. Don't associate with that guy. He's a major turn-off." A major turn off? That's like saying Hitler was "naughty." She was preaching to the choir.

I had given up my portion of the producer's fee to Mr. Unnamed, and I got Leslie involved in the first place. I needed this lawyer jerk like I needed fifth-stage syphilis. Come to think of it, the syphilis would probably have been preferable. I had to be the one to buy back my own script in order to "hide" Mr. Unnamed's involvement with Disney. But the worst was yet to come.

Disney has many unbreakable policies, one of which is to never pay over "quote" to any actor, director, writer, or producer. This quote is the fee paid on the last movie the actor, director, writer, or producer did.

Leslie's agent was asking for a quarter of a million dollars over what he made on Mel Brooks's ***Dracula,*** which tanked in a week. Disney wouldn't budge on Leslie's salary demand. Our co-producer genius, who started courting Leslie like a teen in heat, came up with a solution: Make Leslie executive producer and pay him the difference.

It was my worst nightmare. Leslie was given a lavish office he never used, a motor home the size of a three-bedroom house, his own craft service person and catering wagon, his own makeup person, hair stylist, and wardrobe designer—and he was given input into casting decisions.

As a cartoon bubble in *MAD Magazine* would say, "Yech!!!"

These days, everyone is in free fall, not realizing the development and production processes of the business model have changed. Studios no longer have a retinue of private investor groups, loyal foreign distributors, and their own pot of hedge fund cash to spend hiring writers, acquiring screenplays, and making movies. It's up to everyone now to find a way to make things less expensively and find some way to interest the few "one percenters" to invest in this huge gamble. But there *is* an upside: many fewer "notes" from a pool of MBAs with little to no practical experience that drive you crazy with their ideas on how to make your script better and who to cast in the movie so it can be green lit.

You are in charge of your destiny. Believe and trust in no one until, as one friend once told me, "I never think my movie is going to be made until I get my breakfast off the craft service truck on the final day of shooting."

RULE # 21:

CASTING IS MORE DIFFICULT THAN CHOOSING A SPOUSE

Since ***Spy Hard*** was a James Bond spoof, we needed first and foremost to cast the female spy to become Leslie's James Bondian love interest. These lady spies are, in the real Bond films, exotic, sexy, and, most often, of foreign nationalities. I wanted a slightly-over-the-hill ex-sexpot who was funny, but sexpot and funny don't necessarily go together. I wanted a real actress. Better yet, I wanted an actress who possibly had been a Bond girl.

My first choice was Joanna Lumley. She had been a Bond girl. She was the sarcastically funny alcoholic co-star in the hilarious British comedy TV series *Absolutely Fabulous*. But she was doing a play in London and was unavailable.

Next on my list was Lena Olin, who's incredibly sexy and beautiful and is an amazing actress. She's also married to one of my director idols, Lasse Hallström (***What's Eating Gilbert Grape*** and ***The Cider House Rules***). She read the script and asked to see my TV commercial demo. She agreed to do the part for six hundred thousand dollars. Disney said, "*Lena Who?!!*"

Disney wouldn't pay that kind of money to any female co-star—even Pamela Anderson wearing a thong . . . especially Pamela Anderson wearing a thong. They were Disney. Pamela Anderson would be fine. But a thong? Walt would turn over in his grave, or cryogenic chamber, or wherever he's enshrined.

In Studio Land, casting's about marquee value. To studio geniuses, like the people working with me, getting butts in theater seats is the only consideration. After all, their MBA taught them nothing about what goes into a movie, only what may dictate profits. To them, the most important part of casting a movie is to cast someone who has been in a hit movie.

I never forget that it was some studio genius—like the ones working for me—that cast Diana Ross, well into her forties, as Dorothy, the nine-year-old-girl lead in the movie ***The Wiz***.

Leslie Nielsen was one of those put-butts-in-theater-seats men—he proved it with the outstanding box office sales of ***The Naked Gun***. We couldn't afford any other butts-in-the-seats actors on our limited budget. Leslie would be our only one, and we were okay with that despite the fact that we had to run our casting choices by him.

I was running out of time and patience. My casting agent and I brainstormed a list of women in their forties who still had great sex appeal. Before the TV series *Desperate Housewives*, a woman over forty couldn't even be considered for a sexy female movie lead despite this being a summer wide release that was funny. Among our options were Polly Walker, Greta Scacchi, Kelly LeBrock, Jaqueline Bisset, Connie Sellecca, and Cheryl Ladd, all off whom were awesome. But they were either too expensive or not outlandishly funny. Then I remembered working with Nicollette Sheridan on a video I directed for Kenny G. She was sexy, gorgeous, and funny. Ironically, she later co-starred in *Desperate Housewives.*

I sent her casting tape to Leslie. He enjoyed it. Then, fearing the worst, I sent it to my exec at Disney. He liked it even better. He'd held out for Pamela Anderson, the ultimate sex bomb with an international following off the charts. But we couldn't afford her even if I agreed to cast her. Our exec was voted Nerd of the Year and was from the Midwest and could have been the model for John Cusack's character in ***The Sure Thing***—-which co-starred Nicollette, making her a shoe-in!

We tweaked the script for Nicollette's character. She was much younger than Leslie. She was funny, a good actress, and a natural tomboy. Her scenes that required kickboxing were amazing. The stunt coordinator said, "She's as good as they come."

Rounding out this gut-wrenching process was casting the bad guy. We had originally named him Doc Martens, after the trendy shoes but Disney refused to negotiate the use of the shoe manufacturer's "product placement," I think because they thought them associated with punk rockers and other demons of American decadence.

I wanted to stay true to the Bond formula. The bad guy is an imperious foreigner. I had my favorites: Patrick Stewart (***Star Trek***); Nigel Hawthorne, academy nominee from ***The Madness of King George***; Academy Award–winner Ben Kingsley (***Gandhi***); multi-award winning Christopher Plummer (***The Girl with the Dragon Tattoo***); and Rutger Hauer (***Blade Runner***).

My exec at Disney invited my manager and me to lunch at the executive dining room atop the Disney executive building. The building's facade displays giant statues of the seven dwarfs from ***Snow White.*** Need I say more? I was in 'Toonville.

"We're not making a Shakespearean repertory movie," he said. "Cast some *Americans.* Get some guys who used to be TV stars. Forget these foreigners." I was beginning to truly hate this snit. He had previously been more of a gnat. Now he was a giant horse fly.

When first speaking with the head of casting for Disney, I told her I wanted Stevie Wonder or Ray Charles to play the part of the bus driver in the ***Speed*** spoof. She looked at me like I just told her her teenage daughter was pregnant. To say she didn't get it is the understatement of the year.

Days later, having cast some incredible actors, rumors about the movie were floating around Disney. The head of casting phoned me and said, "I get it. I'm so sorry. I thought you were out of your mind. Go. Stevie Wonder or Ray Charles."

Though these actors have all become superstars, can you imagine ***This Boy's Life*** without the young unknown Leonardo diCaprio? Or ***Easy Rider*** without the obscure Jack Nicholson? Or the far-from-famous Al Pacino missing in ***The Godfather***? Or anyone but the young Dustin Hoffman in ***The Graduate***? Or Meryl Streep absent from her early role in ***The French Lieutenant's Woman***? Or ***Edward Scissorhands*** without not-yet-star Johnny Depp? Or ***The Professional*** without the unknown teenager Natalie Portman? Or ***Winter's Bone*** without the incredible young then-unknown-now-***Hunger Games, Silver Linings Playbook*** and ***American Hustle***-star Jennifer Lawrence?

All of them acted in *something* before these break-out roles. But they exhibited the perfect persona that writers and directors sought. It is essential to cast the most appropriate actor that can add artistry to your script and to the vision of your film.

If you give serious thought to choosing a mate/spouse, what do you look for? First: character. Well, that's already in your screenplay. In casting, you seek the actor that most fulfills that character. Second: attractiveness. I can't imagine most people *not* attracted to the person they chose as a mate. And let's face it, audiences want to be attracted to a lead character in a movie or TV show. Third: humor. You wouldn't want a humorless spouse, would you? And in the movies, even if the role is a dramatic one, its fun to work with someone who has a sense of humor. But finally, there are a couple traits necessary to choosing a mate/spouse that we just don't have time to look for while casting: honesty and loyalty. When casting an actor, one can't have *everything*. And after all, they're playing a role.

RULE # 22:

MAKING MOVIES MAY NOT BE BRAIN SURGERY, BUT IT SURE NEEDS EXPERIENCED SURGEONS

It is time for diversity to be standard procedure for hiring anyone in any position in the entertainment business. Every guild recognizes the need to disband the white boys' club but, despite growing appreciation for cultural and sexual diversity, the prevalence of ageism in Hollywood is one of its biggest downfalls. Artists, craftspeople, actors, writers, and directors with lengthy lists of award-winning credits are never considered for work by young producers and studio execs. It's these "up-and-comers" greatest fault and their greatest loss. Movies are a collaborative medium. To have experienced people watch your back is a godsend. You surely wouldn't want a first-year medical student operating on your brain.

Why would any major league sports team draft a no-name from college instead of a pitcher with the lowest ERA or a hitter with the highest batting average? But I guess in the film industry, it must have something to do with the core audience of wide release movies—fourteen- to twenty-four-year-olds. I think studios believe that writers, directors, and actors in their twenties know so much more about teenagers than more experienced, older veterans just because they're closer in age.

An argument against this misconception could be made with the example of Academy Award–winning ***Brokeback Mountain***, which was based on a short story and adapted by a man and woman well into their sixties. Do these young MBA types believe that either Anne Proulx or Larry

McMurtry ever hung out with young gay cowboys so that they'd be the perfect fit to write about them?

One well-known rumor concerned the director of the hilarious heist comedy ***A Fish Called Wanda***, co-written by and starring John Cleese. He had chosen Charles Crichton, director of one of the legendary heist comedies of history, ***The Lavender Hill Mob***. As a man in his late seventies, the studio wouldn't hire him for love or money. So Cleese said he would direct. Then he let Crichton do the job, thereby allowing this "old man" to do the bang-up job he did and receive the directing credit he deserved.

When deciding whom to choose as a production designer for ***Spy Hard***, my line producer, Bob Rosen, who had produced Alex Cox's ***The Crow***, asked me, "Do you have anything against hiring an older person?" I responded, "Absolutely not." Rosen told me, "Then I got the perfect guy for you. Bill Creber."

Bill Creber, in his late seventies, has been inducted in both the Academy of Motion Pictures and the Production Designer's Guild with a lifetime achievement award. He was nominated for Academy Awards for ***The Poseidon Adventure*** and ***The Towering Inferno***.

When I met Bill, he showed me a copy of our script. On the back of dozens of pages were sketches of some of the sets, props, and designs that occurred to him as he read it. One of which was the chair in which Charles Durning would hide. I was so impressed, I hired him on the spot.

Charles Durning's character, as head of The Agency, is depicting his attempts at being a spy instead of an administrator. He tries different tricks to hide himself within the Agency, as a field spy would. Leslie Nielsen, a.k.a. Dick Steele, is called into the director's office to be briefed on finding a captured female agent. Durning, the director, is nowhere to be found. Leslie looks everywhere. He gives up and sits in a leather armchair. True to Leslie's personal humor, he cuts a signature fart (he was known for the small squeeze machine he carried in his palm). The back head cushion of the chair flips up, revealing Durning hiding inside the chair, who exclaims, "Geez, Steele, what'd you have for lunch?!"

Leslie, surprised, jumps out of the chair. Durning stands, with the various parts of the chair velcroed to his body, and removes them one by one, while he briefs Leslie. Building this chair was one of many incredible feats dreamed up by Creber.

We had no money and no time for CGI—they took much longer and were much more expensive. Everything we did had to be old school: split screens, miniatures, and set pieces that would trick the eye.

The most innovative scene designed by Creber was the rooftop sequence we shot to parody the movie ***True Lies***. In the original movie, Arnold Schwarzenegger rides horseback into an elevator to the rooftop of a skyscraper while being chased by the bad guy, who's riding a motorcycle. When reproducing a scene in parody, I always attempt to stay as close to the original as possible. Therefore, we shot Leslie Nielsen riding a horse through the same lobby of the old Ambassador Hotel as Arnold had. He then enters an elevator, on horseback, as Arnold did.

Then came Creber's tour de force. He designed and built two faux elevators atop a parking garage and a faux parapet surrounding three sides of the garage rooftop. As Leslie, on horseback, exits one elevator, our bad guy exits the other elevator and gives chase. Leslie rides full bore across the roof and skids to a stop before the horse falls over the edge. Fortunately for animal lovers, the horse "falls" into a swimming pool, one floor down. This was done by split screening, with the broken parapet in the foreground and an overhead shot of the Ambassador's swimming pool with the horse already swimming in it.

Leslie next appears, as Arnold did, at the pilot's controls of a Harrier jet. Creber borrowed the fiberglass Harrier jet mock-up used in ***True Lies***. The jet was attached to a cable, and then we lifted it up over our parapet, by a crane, with Leslie in the pilot's seat. Leslie jumps out of the jet, onto our parapet, and escapes. In post-production, we removed the cable from the scene digitally. This entire sequence was shot in one day for $200,000. The original cost three million and took a week's shooting.

That was just one instance concerning a man in his late seventies who knew more about methods of achieving "Movie Magic" than almost everyone younger than he. My suggestion to anyone who has to find a creative/technical person to perform an unusual or highly critical function: Do not close your mind to anyone, no matter their age.

* * * *

Although "behind the scenes" snippets of movies and television production run on YouTube, *Entertainment Tonight* and ancillary material on DVDs, there is nothing like seeing a movie being shot. First-time witnesses of movie shoots can never believe the number of people, vehicles, and gear that goes into creating something an ordinary audience member would see on TV or in a theatre.

The final night of the shoot on ***Spy Hard***, we were to shoot the bus-driving part of the ***Speed*** parody. Nicollette Sheridan's character has saved Leslie's character's life, and they are now a pair, running to hop on a bus, fleeing their pursuers. The bus driver is Ray Charles.

We rented the bus from the man who modified it for ***Speed***. The actual driver drove from atop the bus, but shooting from inside, it looked like Ray was driving. We shot on Hollywood Boulevard, right before Christmas. The lights decorating the boulevard would add production value to what one sees through the bus windows from inside. The bus was filled with extras as passengers. I sat in the rearmost seat, hunkered down to hide my headset and portable monitor.

Ray Charles, driving the bus, approaches Leslie and Nicollette, who are waiting at the bus stop. During the shoot, I looked out the window to see, walking toward the bus along the boulevard, three overlarge women in sweat suits, looking as if they were tourists, straight out of Branson, Missouri.

The bus came to a stop to admit Leslie and Nicolette. The doors opened, revealing Ray, in a tux, wearing sunglasses, in the driver's seat. I looked at the sweat-suited women's reaction. Had they had false teeth, they'd have fallen out. They were so surprised, they looked at each other as if E.T. had just landed. Leslie and Nicollette boarded. The door closed. We drove off. I saw the women standing still, in shock. I'm sure they rushed back to their tour bus and screamed, "Take us to the airport! Hollywood's filled with maniacs!" No, it's filled with incredible artists and technicians, some of whom have taken several decades to learn what they know.

* * * *

My producer friend Larry Franco, who worked as assistant director on the epic ***Apocalypse Now***, told me how he staged the 'background' in the iconic helicopters/napalm war scene in the movie. He divided legions of extras into large groups, just like the military would, and he assigned a small crew of explosive, pyrotechnic (fire and smoke), special effects, stunt people, and safety officers to each group. He named each group with a name of a color. In each group there was a second assistant director, who would take orders from Larry over walkie-talkie. Knowing in advance where the helicopters would fly and where the camera placements would be, Larry could then cue each group to fire their explosives, leap in the air, and throw up dummies calling out their color moniker, so that the final shot would be timed to look authentic in its progression. Obviously, those that have seen the movie most likely would agree that it was one of the most impressive war scenes ever filmed. Whether or not they like the smell of napalm in the morning.

Brain surgeons are not born, they're made. They're made by learning their craft from experienced teachers and mentors over time and through experience. That necessary time and experience applies to anyone with any skill in show business.

RULE # 23:

YOUR CREW WILL WALK OVER NAILS FOR YOU WHEN YOU TREAT THEM AS FAMILY

I was asked to direct an ad campaign for AAMI Insurance in Australia. The company loved Chevy Chase and in the tradition of his ***Vacation*** movies, they hired Chevy to re-create his role. They hired me to helm a campaign that was intended to impress the viewers with the fact that AAMI would insure any mishap.

The Australians I met were like the people I grew up with in Cheyenne. They joked a lot and cared nothing for class nor stature. The producer, who I had known in L.A, was a woman named Lizzy Nash, and she is one of my favorite producers. She leaves no detail overlooked and finds no job too exacting, and no one is more fun than she is—she's an Aussie.

The first thing I attempt to learn on any shoot is everybody's name, thereby showing respect to those who will bring me through the war of making a film. Secondly, I give praise where praise is due. The actors and crew people are doing their best to deliver what they think I expect from them. Lastly, I accept advice. My credo is: If there's a better way to build this mousetrap, I'll take it. Following these three tenets and creating an atmosphere of esprit de corps will ensure your film family will kick ass for you. And most important: Keep a feeling of fun. I like to find those crew and cast people I can joke with, and then I kid the hell out of them.

I looked forward to working with Chevy. After watching him on *Saturday Night Live*, he was one of my favorite comics. His greeting on the *SNL* news said it all: "Good evening. I'm Chevy Chase, and you're not." In real life, he was like the friends I grew up with, unafraid to make a fool of himself. He'd come up with twelve lame jokes before he hit a gold mine.

I first met Chevy in the Ritz-Carlton Hotel. "This is the exact suite in which Michael Hutchence died," the producer told him. Hutchence, lead singer of the famous rock group INXS, allegedly hung himself in an autoerotic belt-hanging error. HOLD IT! Hung himself in an autoerotic belt-hanging error? What is *that*?! He was making love to his belt hanging on a hook in the closet? No matter how many years I've lived in Hollywood, I still can't believe there are sexual acts *that* weird. I'm from Cheyenne, where *auto* means car and *erotic* means porno magazines wrapped in plastic so you can't flip through them and stare at larger-than-imaginable private parts, and hanging yourself with your own belt for sexual gratification could only happen to the dumbest fool on earth.

Chevy's grinning response to all this: "Really?" He then proceeded to place things for the maids that would make them think twice. He hung a belt from the header beam, wrapped a towel around his neck like a noose, and had us take a snapshot that he then scotch-taped to the bathroom mirror.

The flagship commercial featured Chevy with a wife and two teenagers driving through the streets of Sydney. Because Australians drive on the left side of the road, Chevy, undaunted, would create havoc as he drove on the right side of the road. In the commercial, a bicyclist swerves to avoid Chevy and is forced up a driveway, hitting an opening car door and flying out of the frame. Chevy's droll comment: "Gee, must be his first time on a bike."

Chevy's next stunt is to drive into an intersection. He doesn't stop, causing the other three cars approaching the intersection to slam on their brakes and go into a skid. Chevy is blind as a bat. He wears thick glasses, but I had him drive without glasses because we had to light him in the car to balance the bright light outside. His eyeglasses would have caused major reflections, so he removed them.

We set up to shoot the intersection stunt. Chevy noticed I had a stunt driver, dressed like him, to drive his station wagon. "Nah," he said, "let me do it. I've done thousands of stunts." I was elated. One of the three cameras we needed to shoot the stunt could now shoot a closer shot of Chevy instead of a stunt driver—more verisimilitude.

I yelled out, "Everybody ready?" and I got a thumbs-up from everyone. Chevy hit the gas and started toward the intersection. The other three drivers started so that they could time their figure eight just as he was in their midst. Chevy made it through just as the three cars smashed the hell out of each other. Chevy stopped his car past the intersection, jumped out, and yelled, "Okay! Everybody ready for take two?"

We split a gut laughing. How the hell could there be a take two with two of the cars already wrecked before they should have been? It was a shining moment. It assured the insurance company that we had something on film that proved they covered any type of accident. Pure gold.

The final shot of the commercial started close on Chevy and the family inside the wagon and then craned up and away as Chevy said, "God I love this country." The camera cranes further away, revealing Chevy had just driven through a pyramid of wrecked cars stacked above his car. Behind the pyramid, we see an entire block of cars up on lawns and stacked atop one another, and the bicyclist hanging upside down from a lamppost.

We were a film family. We ate outdoors, barbeque style, with crew people sitting with "above the line" people. The lack of social hierarchy was refreshing and, again, reminiscent of Cheyenne. I treated everyone on this job the same way I treat everyone on every job, like they are members of my own family, and I expect from them the same respect, aid, and comfort that I give them. The result was not only a terrific commercial campaign, but also a fun, fulfilling experience because I was able to bond with everyone who worked on the shoot. And that's the way it should be on every shoot.

If you're interested in watching the Chevy Chase TV commercial, find it on YouTube at:

http://www.youtube.com/watch?v=LvykBWVq-c0

RULE # 24:

WHEN SHOOTING IN A FOREIGN LOCATION, REMEMBER *YOU* ARE THE FOREIGNER

Spy Hard was number one at the box office in Germany for a month. I received a phone call from Jacques Steyn, a producer in Germany, who asked, "Do you want to do a commercial for Germany?" "Does it pay American money?" I flippantly asked.

After directing the commercials for Jacques, he introduced me to a production company in Paris. I directed three campaigns for them. For almost three years I was out of the country—in France, Germany, Italy, Spain, Venezuela, and Australia—directing TV commercials. Once the ad agency "bought" your vision of the commercial, they allowed you to shoot what you wanted, and they actually paid you to supervise the edit, unlike in America.

French movies have always impressed me. Not just the narrative kind like ***The Artist*** or ***Amour*** but also the documentaries, like ***Man on a Wire***, the docu-drama trek ***Himalaya***, and the extraordinary ***March of the Penguins***. With that movie, a small group of visionaries spent months, even years, capturing a story that should go into a time capsule.

I directed two successful TV commercial campaigns in Paris; they were shown on French TV and in theaters before the movies began. One was a spoof of James Bond, the other of Frankenstein.

Twix Candy "Frankenstein"

The French are different from anyone else on this planet. I challenge anyone to explain to me how this imperialistic, materialistic, fashionistic country came to be known as so socially and egalitarian minded. But I guess accent is everything.

After script and casting, preparation is the most important element in filmmaking. Quoting a co-worker: "If it ain't on the page, it ain't on the stage." I need the finished film in my mind before I shoot it. I need to approve every prop, piece of wardrobe, set design, and special effect. For the Frankenstein commercial, I researched all the sets and props from the original movies. I photographed the Strickfaden electrical gadgets, like the Jacob's Ladder, which electrical waves could climb. I sent these photos to the production designer in Paris to recreate.

The production designer hired a pair of older prop men who created the most amazing props and set decorations. This commercial was a *MAD Magazine*–style look at Dr. Frankenstein's lab. In addition to the recognizable movie props, I wanted vintage torture devices, barber chairs, medical implements—any period hardware that was funny.

In the commercial, the monster's head is severed from his body. It sits upon a sterling silver carving platter adjacent to the medical autopsy table, upon which the body lies. The good Doctor F. watches television on a vintage brass-riveted Jules Verne TV set. On the TV runs stock footage of butchers in the old Les Halles market, hacking large animal carcasses to pieces with meat cleavers.

I had to wait while the TV was being built. I asked, "Why wasn't all this finished before I got here?!" The producer merely chortled that condescending way French people do when speaking to crazy Americans, "We work as we go," and he added in his head, *You American idiot.* Sure enough, everything was finished the moment it was needed.

The same ad agency then asked me to shoot a spot for Mars Ice Cream. It was winter, and they wanted an excuse to go to the tropics and catch some rays. This time I was to do a spoof of ***Knife in the Water***, Roman Polanski's epic.

To keep the budget low, they chose to go to Venezuela. We ferried in a vintage sailboat, the one Brad Pitt languished on in ***Legends of the Fall***—a restored 1920s teak beauty—magnifique.

Because French residual payments weren't required for foreigners, we cast actors from New York. The young male was everyman funny. The female was gorgeous with a killer body, that year's Wonderbra girl. Most important, she exuded a French kind of attitude. The last decisions to be made were to hire a Venezuelan production service to fill out the crew, rent the places to stay, and rent motor boats to take us to the "picture" sail boat.

We stayed in Morrocoy, a coastal resort four hours from Caracas, and we drove over mountains in vans that should have been junked instead of driven to get to the location. Dozens of Venezuelan crew piled out of the vans. I'm not sure what they did. The Venezuelan production service employed as many family members as they could fit in the van. A few of them probably knew something about film, but most likely it was only the part of "audience member." We brought the bikinis from Paris and a hand-crafted vintage icebox to match the deco boat's interior. We just needed a few extra bodies to wrangle lighting gear and mount the icebox in the boat.

The owner of the picture boat and his girlfriend stayed on the boat, moored a half hour out into the water. They spoke German and a little English. The Frenchies spoke French and a little less English. The Venezuelans spoke only Spanish. I speak just enough French, Spanish, and German to be dangerous. To the ad agency and production company guys' delight, the Wonderbra girl, having been a top runway model in Paris, spoke fluent French.

In the first shot of the commercial, we had to establish the couple languishing on the boat. I wanted to start the camera from water level so we could include the vintage carved-wood, female Neptune on the bow of the boat, tilt up, and travel along the side of the boat to reveal our two actors.

We affixed the camera to a kind of mini-crane we mounted on a piece of plywood atop a small motorboat. We could then crane up from water level as we motored by the side of the picture boat. But in every take, the skiff's driver would veer away from the course I'd set. I asked him nicely, "*Por favor, Señor. Vaya mas cerca al barco.*" Go closer to the boat. He'd smile and nod, "*De accuerdo.*" Then he'd make the same mistake time after time. I think the production service made sure to hire boats that didn't leak, not necessarily captains that could drive a boat well—sort of like a baseball team hiring players based on how nice their mitts are.

Finally, one of the Frenchies pointed out the problem. The picture boat was tied off at each end in the water to keep it stable. These ties were long ropes, and they were barely submerged. The driver of our boat didn't want to catch his propeller in the tie-off rope. I turned to my producer and told him, "Get some sandbags and make the tie-off rope sink deeper." The producer called out: "Sandbags!" Instantly, a dozen sandbags, which are sewn together in the middle so they could be draped over a line, appeared. We dropped them along the tie-off rope, and it sunk into the water enough to clear the propeller and get us our shot.

We wrapped at dark, jumped in a rowboat, made it to shore, and piled into our vans to return to the motel. One of our two vans departed, carrying the two actors and the Venezuelans. In the second van, we went fifty feet before running out of gas.

We spied a rusty old pickup coming toward us. I jumped out and asked the driver, "*Puede usted llevarnos a Morrocoy*?" Can you take us to Morrocoy? The producer instantly produced a handful of cash. The driver, an old man with half his teeth missing, smiled and answered, "*De accuerdo*!" I yelled to the boat, "*Rufen sie das hotel mit ihrem radio. Fragen sie unserer crew zum zurück kommen*!" What I hoped I said was, "Use your ship radio to call the hotel. Tell them to come back to pick us up." I knew this ratty old truck would take forever to make the drive.

We set off on the road. The driver, cinematographer, and I rode in the cab, the ad agency twosome and French producer in the pickup bed. I thought to myself, *I'll never work for these guys again.* The pickup traveled at the speed of a small dog. To add insult, whenever the driver spotted someone walking along the road, he'd slow down and converse and laugh with them, most likely making fun of us.

I vented, "Where the hell's the other van?!" Still creeping along in the pickup, we finally saw a van barreling toward us. We hopped in the other van and told the driver to drive as fast as he could. I can now relate to *The*

Amazing Race. This shoot tested my patience and perseverance. But I did learn a lesson: I was the foreigner in a foreign land.

If your script calls for a foreign location, or more commonly, if financing dictates it (Romania is the current fav of producers trying to stretch their limited budgets), be prepared. Prepare for more than just making films. And prepare to encounter obstacles you'd never dream of encountering in America, especially Hollywood. And remember, things you assume are natural in America don't always apply in a foreign land.

If you're interested in watching the Frankenstein TV commercial, find it on YouTube at:

http://www.youtube.com/watch?v=78n4

And if you're interested in watching the Mars Ice Cream TV commercial, find it at:

http://www.youtube.com/watch?v=9vf17sQFWdw

RULE # 25:

THE MOMENT YOU TRUST PEOPLE YOU DON'T KNOW, BE PREPARED FOR THE WORST

My studio exec on ***Spy Hard*** and his boss, president of Disney's Hollywood Pictures, came to the set. I was forewarned by Su Armstrong, our physical production executive, who called and told me, "Rick, the creative team is coming to visit you. They are extremely pleased with your dailies. They want to see what extra jokes you want to shoot." I said, "Great!" She answered, "Not great. The *real* reason they're coming is that you're over budget."

The rig built to turn the presidential limo around, hold it secure, and then release it into the water didn't work. We had to reshoot the scene, putting us one day behind schedule.

I implored her, "What do I do? What do I tell them? Her suggestion: "Make a list of a dozen gags you think you can lose. Fight tooth and nail for them and give up most of them. Keep the ones you know you need." She hung up. I loved this woman!

Most studio execs—the suits—feign support; they try to give you a warm and fuzzy feeling. Mine didn't. He was humorless and colorless, and he became the largest pain in the rear you could imagine.

Spy Hard's agency set was your typical CIA war room. One wall, filled with TV monitors, was labeled "Hot Zones." In each monitor ran news footage of catastrophes, riots, and wars, with the accompanying name of the hot zone below its respective monitor. Newark: shots of looting and burning. North Korea: shots of soldiers goose stepping. Chernobyl: fire and clouds of toxic smoke. Palestine: Jews chasing Palestinians one way, Palestinians chasing them the other. Daytona Beach: chicks in skimpy bikinis spraying dudes with six-pack abs with beer from a keg hose. San Francisco: a clip from ***Reefer Madness***. Poland: a shot I quickly picked up with a home video camera:

I put Chudnow atop a ladder and chose the four largest crew guys to dress in wife beaters and jeans pulled down to show their butt cracks. While Chudnow held onto a lightbulb, they turned the ladder around. Your classic Polish joke.

I received a phone call from my pinhead exec at Disney, who said, "You know my wife is Polish. I don't appreciate that joke."

Was he blind?! We'd made fun of every race, religious creed, sex, age, affliction, and occupation known to man. *This* was a stickler?! This douche bag exec was now a festering boil with the sense of humor of Vladimir Putin. Could it get any worse? Yeah, and it did. Post-production was the abyss. I was in the Temple of Doom.

Spy Hard's opening scene establishes The Agency. Around a semi-circular table sit various spies. Their name plates identify their agencies: CIA, FBI, DEA, ATF, FCC, UJA, NBA, AAA, and YMCA. At the table are cameo players like baseball legend Mike Piazza, former president Clinton's brother Roger Clinton, and the then coach of the L.A. Lakers, Del Harris.

Charles Durning, the head of The Agency, a frustrated spy, pops up from the table, the table top still affixed to his head. He briefs everyone on the bad guy they're after—the evil General Rancor, played by Andy Griffith. They watch a videotape Rancor's sent, showing the agency's kidnapped female spy. Charlie Durning was humble and warm. He was a virtuoso. The scene was priceless. Hilarious. Reminiscent of ***Airplane!***

Disney cut it. The moron executive in charge said it had "too many principles" (meaning too many actors). That reminded me of Salieri's comment about Mozart's symphony in the movie ***Amadeus***: "Too many notes."

What I later learned was that I could demand that this executive be replaced. Since my film was already in production and, allegedly, a big favorite of studio chief Joe Roth, this could have been feasible. But I'd yet to know how truly despicable this little nerd was. I figured, again showing my naivete, better the devil you know . . . Besides, I didn't know where to find a legitimate exorcist.

Fern Champion, my casting friend, told me a director she worked for said, "Making films is not a popularity contest. It's a war. Act accordingly." Most people in Hollywood you meet for the first time on a job—not those on your cast and crew, but the agents, managers, and studio execs—are usually solicitous and respectful. Why not? It's a great insurance policy: If your film hits, you'll remember that kindness. If it doesn't, they never have to speak to you again.

* * * *

Every day during the filming of ***Spy Hard***, we broke for lunch and ate together in the Ambassador Hotel's dining room. After lunch we'd see dailies. It was an open session. As far as I was concerned, if the dailies got laughs, the scenes were funny. During lunch, a team of agents from three of the big agencies—ICM, William Morris, and UTA—came to visit. They seemed like nice folk, and they had all read the script and had heard positive feedback from the studio and the crew. They all told me to come meet their staff when the film wrapped.

I did. William Morris had a room full of people. They asked what I'd like to do next and offered a few suggestions. None of them sounded great. ICM was a smaller group. The point person was married to an assistant director who'd heard nice things about me. She was warm and complimentary. Her boss, the head of the motion picture department, was a wait-and-see kinda guy.

UTA was impressive. Another room full of agents. They'd read the script for ***Spy Hard*** and had seen my TV commercial reel. They had good ideas. The head Disney point man said, "You want to up your game. Become an A player." The head of the agency, said, "The most important thing is not to get into development hell." He meant that I needed to direct a film that was ready to go. "We'll start stirring up the waters with your commercial reel and any excerpt from ***Spy Hard*** as soon as you preview," he added. Then he continued, "If you preview well, word will get out and *everyone* will be on you." The movie would open Memorial Day weekend, one of the plum three-day slots to open youth-oriented movies. They also knew I'd have stiff competition: ***Twister***, ***Striptease***, and ***Mission: Impossible.***

I liked these people. They had a plan. So I decided to sign with them. The agency head told me, "Come to see us after you preview." Little did I know how much would be at stake . . . and how little any of these people gave a damn if I lived or died, as long as my movie was a hit.

When you're the flavor of the week, *everybody* wants to know and befriend you. And they're all nice. For a guy from Cheyenne, "nice" would describe people you want to hang out with. In Hollywood, you have to erase that from your mind. Until you are actually the pick to pop, no one gives a rat's nose who you are or what you've done.

RULE # 26:

DEVELOPMENT IS LIKE SWIMMING UPSTREAM WITHOUT YOUR ARMS

After ***Spy Hard*** and the problems I encountered with my Disney exec (see Rule 28 – Man is not meant to Preview,) I dropped UTA and signed with a younger agent at a smaller agency, APA, who was enthusiastic. He told me, "You're the biggest client I have. I will work for you twenty-four hours a day for a year." He was one of the hardest working agents I'd met, but he was with an agency that had no star writers or directors or actors. In Hollywood, an agent's appeal comes from his or her representing people in demand. No one wants you unless everyone wants you. Nevertheless, the agent did attempt to connect me with the marketplace, which was open to suggestions.

While I was out of the country directing commercials, this new agent fielded inquiries for me to direct broad comedies slated for youths in the summer market. I read eight-dozen scripts—all crap. I turned them all down. Only 10 percent of them got made. They all tanked at the box office. And I then realized what the head of UTA meant when he said "development hell": I accepted three opportunities, through APA, to supervise rewrites of movies that never were made.

Here's how it works: A producer, or a wannabe producer, options a book, story treatment, or screenplay. It may have been written by a produced writer, published author, or the producer's newly-graduated-from-film-school's neice/nephew, son/daughter, or one of the *twenty thousand* writers who fill the Internet with descriptions of their newest idea, treatment, or screenplay.

Said producer then has to "package" the screenplay with an actor and/or director in order to entice a studio to make this movie. Making movies is just like playing tennis, but without the balls—because very few people have them. Anyway, a tennis player always wants to play with someone better than him or herself. The aforementioned producer has to somehow obtain a commitment from a "bankable" star and/or director, or at least someone who currently has or very recently had a movie in theaters.

Having directed a movie, which was still playing at that time, that grossed over $86 million worldwide theatrical, I fell into the category of someone who has a movie currently in theaters. Producers approached me with the above mentioned literary material and either asked me to re-write the material and attach myself to direct it or paid me a nominal fee to attach myself to direct it.

After directing the series of commercials in Australia with Chevy Chase, Chevy and I became friends. My agent had sent me a script written by a client I recommended to him, Mitch Markowitz, who wrote ***Good Morning, Vietnam***. The screenplay was about a happily married advertising exec who is lured into a potential quick affair with a young intern in his agency while his lawyer wife is out of town at a convention. The script is a classic comedy of errors as what would be Chevy's character gets deeper and deeper into trouble trying to bed the intern as her demands escalate.

Chevy liked the script and took it first to Mark Canton, a producer at Warner Brothers Studios, with whom he had worked when Mark shepherded Chevy's legendary hilarious film, ***Caddyshack***. Chevy set up a meeting with Canton to pitch my take on the movie we wanted to make. Canton, flanked by his young development exec who had read and liked the screenplay, never looked me in the eye or called me by name. As I previously mentioned, when someone needs to know you, they refer to you by name. I had no high hopes for Canton's passion about me or our movie.

Because Chevy was insistent, Canton took the script to the co-presidents of Warner, both of whom were Chevy's "friends," Terry Semel and Robert Daly. His ***Vacation*** movies had grossed over half a billion dollars for them. But they passed the project onto a younger executive, Lorenzo di Bonaventura, who has since become one of the most successful and prominent producers in Hollywood (***Salt, Red, Transformers, Jack Ryan***, and a host of others).

Chevy, who has a movie shown on TV every night of the year, somewhere, didn't know that Semel and Daley were on their way out and that Lorenzo would replace them as studio head. Lorenzo's take was that Chevy was "too old" for the current teenage market and that his films didn't do well in foreign markets. Another one down the drain for me.

The commercial campaign in Australia, with Chevy starring, was made because his movies were incredibly popular in *that* foreign country, and I guess they didn't consider him "too old." In keeping with the system's unspoken policy manual, there's always twenty reasons to say no. And most of them are motivated by the fear of making a wrong decision.

Someone told me that development is the equivalent of getting a bank loan or choosing the house special at a Chinese restaurant. You get one from column A (script, credit rating, appetizer), one from column B (star, house appraisal, main course), and one from column C (director, two years of tax statements, desert), and *shazam*! You get your movie/loan/meal. Such is development hell.

RULE # 27:

YOU GET CREDIT OR YOU GET BLAME

The Writers and Directors Guilds have, over many decades, fought tooth and nail for rules and regulations concerning credits as they appear on movie and television screens. Just as important are the rumor mills of Hollywood, where so many people give credit where it isn't due and, much more damaging, blame where it is even less due.

Reality television has taken off like wildfire. Broadcasting stories starring "real" people has become the staple of cable television. Makers of reality television take their medium very seriously. Reality becomes relative. It's drama they're really after. And if that drama invigorates lots of viewers, they take the credit for creating it.

I asked my wife, a reality junkie, "Why the hell do you watch this crap?" "I love watching these people," she answered. "They're all a potential train wreck." I asked her, "Don't you realize there's cameras and microphones everywhere?" She answered, "Yeah, but I think these people just don't give a damn."

My friend, Scott Dunlop, created the reality show *The Real Housewives of Orange County*, set in the largest and most affluent gated community in California, Coto de Caza. They board Arabian horses and have a country club with an Olympic pool, full basketball court, eighteen-hole golf course, and a myriad of tennis courts. The houses range from three to thirty million dollars.

Scott had a friend from New York, who had worked for cable network, Bravo, shoot a teaser. Bravo liked the idea. Scott called me to direct the pilot. After shooting the pilot and segments of the first three shows, I received a letter from the Directors Guild. It read, "You are directing for a non-signatory. You must insist the production company become signatory to the DGA, or you must quit."

I didn't need an excuse to quit. Bravo was coming down hard on Scott to take the funny out and make the show a "fly-on-the-wall documentary." Like there's objectivity in reality TV. People who produce reality shows force situations and confrontations upon the "real" women they follow to ensure something catty will arise when the characters get together. Bravo's core audience is women and gay men, and catty is their métier.

Business as usual: Networks see the participants in these shows as fodder for their profits. The more ridiculous they make the "real" people look, the nicer the producers' suites in Cabo San Lucas will be. They purport to be objective journalists. I seriously doubt *60 Minutes* would hire any of them .

Scott is six foot five, from Indiana, was a college basketball player, and is a successful entrepreneur, former member of the Groundlings comedy troupe, and a formidable statesman. Bravo treated him like a doormat. But he had the only access to the community. He, alone, cast the five women featured in the show, all of whom he'd known socially for years.

The show is the biggest hit in Bravo history. It spawned ten more seasons and spin offs in New York, New Jersey, Atlanta, Washington D.C., Beverly Hills, and Miami. Bravo's popularity grew exponentially, from two million to twenty million viewers. Scott was never mentioned in the numerous articles written about the show, despite his being charismatic—a natural interviewee.

Scott and I spoke about the show's success and the amount of queries he received for press interviews. The question in both our minds was, "Why is this show so popular?" The women were superficial, lousy parents, and shopaholics. My answer: "Half the viewers can feel superior because they hate them. The other half want to *be* them." This covers a huge demographic that reality TV execs yearn for. Viewers can't turn away from a train wreck.

Bravo assigned a "show runner" to mastermind the show's episodes, even though this was a "fly-on-the-wall documentary." He was gay, which helped Bravo with their aim of writing about catty women. But he was delusional thinking that he could fit in in right-wing, homophobic Orange County.

Perhaps because I usually work in comedy, the gay men I have worked with are usually the wittiest and most style-conscious crew members. Not so with this show runner.

The biggest laugh Scott shared with me concerned the show runner. Scott told me, "This show runner wants to meet with Matt. He thinks they have a lot in common." Matt was married to the most central housewife, an ex-playboy Playmate I had directed in a bit part in ***Off the Wall*** when her name was Jeana Tomasina, the girl in the ZZ Top music video, *She's got legs*. Once married, with grown children, to Matt, her name is Jeana Keough, though she's since divorced.

Matt was formerly a professional baseball player. He pitched for the Anaheim Angels and Oakland Athletics. He had to retire when he was hit in the head by a fly ball while sitting in the dugout. Matt was the last person the show runner would want to meet. The reason he told Scott that he thought he and Matt would get along was, "We're both small-town boys from the Midwest." The show runner was small, never played sports, and was as bland as vanilla. Matt was big and bombastically opinionated with no patience for anyone he wouldn't consider a "real man."

Scott was so depressed about the way the network treated him, he was nearly inconsolable. I tried to make him laugh. I explained to him my theory about Hollywood: "It's all about credit and blame. If the show hits, they take the credit. If it tanks, you take the blame."

This is akin to the parable about the scorpion and the frog: The scorpion hitches a ride across a river on the back of a frog. Before they land, the scorpion stings the frog, and they drown. With his dying words the frog asks, "Why did you sting me?" The scorpion answers, "Because it's in my nature." So goes the ways of Hollywood. It's in their nature to backstab, and they would say it just as matter-of-factly as the scorpion.

The head of NBC's alternative programming, himself gay and first to tell you so, takes credit for creating *The Real Housewives of Orange County*. He even has his own show about the show. The business affairs executive told Scott, "I really envy you." Scott was incredulous and exclaimed, " What?!!!" The exec explained, "You're the last person standing." (from the original show's staff.)

Success in Hollywood makes for an atmosphere of fear, envy and jealousy. The suits will take advantage of you while smiling in your face, telling you how much they *love* your work.

Reality television is about conceiving and manipulating reality. If it's successful and people watch it in droves, someone else will take all the credit they can. If it fails, whether or not you are at fault, good luck on your next job because no matter how good a job you did, *you* take the blame.

RULE # 28:

MAN IS NOT MEANT TO PREVIEW

With most movies, especially comedies, there are methods of pre-testing audience reaction. Previews are arranged by a market research firm. They hire college students to hand out free tickets to a new movie. The first thing to know is which primary audience the film is intended to reach. We thought the core audience for ***Spy Hard*** was junior high–through college-aged, primarily male, youths.

The research company is given the mandate to profile their intended audience before they solicit them. Our favorite nerdling executive gave the mandate to hand tickets out to the widest possible audience. His claim to fame was ***The Santa Clause***, with TV sitcom actor Tim Allen, which had broad appeal to young and old, male and female viewers. *Not* our audience.

Besides assessing the audience's overall response, there is another upside to previewing. One gains insight into which jokes work best. You simply put a microphone and recorder in the back of the theater and record the laughter in sync with the film. That's normal. Professional. But ours was a cluster fuck. Our previewing audience ranged from little old ladies in their seventies to little kids below the age of eight. I sat there with my stomach churning. The only thing I could gauge was the laughter and comments from a group of male youths. They even laughed at all the 'back-of-the-room' jokes—signage, set decoration, graffiti, and extras doing gags. I knew, if this was an indication, the eventual intended *paying* audience would indeed enjoy this film.

The market research firm reports findings based upon cards filled out by the entire audience as well as the results of a smaller focus group from the audience. On the cards, audience members are asked to list what they liked and disliked about the film. The cards are collated and summarized the following day by the research company. The focus group is held right after the film, and only people who desire to be a part of it are encouraged to stay behind. After the findings are recorded, they're compiled into a report that is presented to the studio, and the first page of the report is a disclaimer:

> It should be kept in mind that an audience survey is not necessarily predictive of box-office success. While the survey can provide information on how well a movie satisfies an audience interested in seeing it (playability), it should not be used to gauge how large the potential audience might be, i.e., it cannot assess the "want to see" level within the broad moviegoer market (marketability.)

They could just as easily claim: "Dating is not necessarily predictive of marriage success. While dating can provide information on how well two people get along in an artificial situation, it should not be used to gauge how successful the marriage might be, i.e., it cannot assess the "want to stay married" level within the broad meat market."

The first preview was pretty much a failure. The comments from the focus group read as if these people had suddenly been elevated to film critics. Some of the comments were ludicrous.

A few scenes of the film were shot on green screen, a special effects process where the green behind the characters gets replaced by a scene of a town, a waterfall, a cliff—as if the characters were actually in that scene. We had not yet composited these scenes with the intended backgrounds, leaving the green background in during the preview, so it was difficult for a layman to tell what we had in mind. Several of these "critics" said, "I didn't like those green scenes." *Duh*—the point of making 'movie magic' is to convince an audience they are perceiving authenticity. They were seeing Leslie and Nicollette against a solid green background—ridiculous!

I did gain insight into scenes that needed to go. This kind of film needs to be short. Jim Abrahams, director of ***Hot Shots! Part Deux***, told my favorite numbskull exec that all of the Zucker, Abrahams and Zucker spoof comedies were eighty-four minutes long, including end credits. We previewed at just under a hundred minutes, not including credits.

Not knowing the ropes buried me. I thought my job was to make this film as good as it could be. I didn't know that most of my time should be spent watching my own back—cutting the bad guys off before they came through the pass.

Spy Hard had a second free preview. I still didn't get the audience I requested. Something started to smell, especially when I was introduced to Jim Abrahams. He'd been invited at the behest of my dickwad executive, who used Jim's previous association with Joe Roth to curry favor. Not only that, my "dear friend," the unnamed needle-dicked co-producer, invited a well-known producer to accompany him. This was a big no-no for Disney, who wanted no outsiders to see the film before it was finished. The summary of the market research group said it all:

> *Spy Hard* generated a relatively good response among the younger (under twenty-four) male audience members, consisting of an above-average "excellent" rating and "definite" recommend scores.

> However, interest among the remaining sex/age groups was lackluster and responded similarly to those in the previous preview. Younger males were generally the strongest levels to date.

The report confirmed my suspicions. My core audience, males of high school and college age, loved it. I was livid.

The following day, my assistant informed me he had been at a sushi bar after the preview. Unbeknownst to the evil dog-licking co-producer, my assistant overheard him telling his successful producer buddy and everyone within earshot how terrible the film was and how horrendous a job I'd done with it.

I immediately took action. I phoned my lawyer and told him what happened. He phoned Disney. The in-house Disney lawyer said he would have my co-producer banned from any future involvement. But the order would have to come from me—it would have to be my idea and my demand. It was too "sticky" for the Disney lawyer to handle himself—he had to have a hitman do it for him. But I had no problem with that, and I had the co-producer banned from future involvement.

I got a call from Chudnow, from Milwaukee, where he lived. He told me, "Jim Abrahams called me. Said our exec offered him the job of completing the film if they replaced you, Rick." Abrahams turned him down, telling Chudnow, "I'd never do that to you guys. Besides, it looks great. It's just too long. Cut it down to eighty-four minutes."

Previews are helpful to improve a movie. But, if you don't have the full support of the studio behind you, that preview can be your and/or your movie's death knell. I have never heard of any movie previewing perfectly to its intended audience. The purpose is to find out where the logic holes may be, which scenes don't "play" in the place they're intended. Then you can fix these problems and make a better movie.

The challenge is ensuring that *everyone* involved in the process has perspective, has experience in previewing, and, most of all, is behind you in wanting to make the best film from what you shot.

RULE # 29:

IF YOU DON'T HAVE A NOSE FOR TREACHERY, NO PROSTHETICS MAKER CAN HELP YOU

By Directors Guild contract, I had ten weeks after completing principle photography to finish my director's cut of ***Spy Hard***. At the insistence of my exec, I handed in an eighty-page list of edits, modifications, additions, voice-overs, superimposed title jokes, and a new spoof of ***Mission: Impossible***, knowing the original was slated to be released the same weekend as ***Spy Hard***.

I went to a meeting to present this to my exec and his boss, the president of Hollywood Pictures, Disney's lower-budget division. Before I could read through my list of changes, my exec surprised me with two documents—lists of suggested changes written by the writers of ***The Santa Clause*** and by his friend who had directed cheesy Saturday morning children's TV shows and who also just happened to be a client of my manager.

I sucked it up, found a few jokes from each document funny, and said so. Then I read through my changes to a totally silent room.

The following morning I received a phone call from my exec. He said, "Rick, the studio is taking over your movie." I was aghast, "Are you kidding me?! That's the most despicable thing I've ever heard!" He coninued, "It's nothing personal. The movie has to have a broad audience." I was enraged, "Charles, our audience is youths between junior high and college age, primarily male. Always was. Always will be." He was unfazed, "We want every movie we make to sell as many tickets as we can." I was fed up, "You're making the biggest mistake of your life."

Nothing personal? I guess that's true of Hollywood—nothing *is* personal. Calling it cold or cruel is like calling Bashar al-Assad mischievous. No relationship is as important as the current project.

I called my lawyer. He promised, "I'll see what I can do." What I didn't know is that I was fireproof. By Directors Guild contract, if you direct 90 percent of principle photography, you cannot be replaced. I'd directed 100 percent. My lawyer scheduled a meeting with the head of business affairs (the same lawyer who agreed to ban the "co-producer" if I ordered it), and my exec. The first thing out of my lawyer's mouth was, "We're not going to exercise our DGA rights." I didn't know at the time what my DGA rights were, but I was sure they must have meant *something*.

"Instead," he continued, "Rick wants to be apprised of everything going on and to have due consideration given to his views." The other two suits looked at each other and nodded, "Of course. We love Rick. The studio just wants to ensure the movie garners the largest audience possible."

Double talk. I'd prefer someone chewing tobacco, spitting to the side, and saying, "Ready when you are, pardner." And we'd draw our six guns. I slipped into a coma. I can't remember another word spoken. I'd been sold out, stabbed in the back, given the shiv, shown the door, submarined with absolutely no reason given and without any restitution possible.

My lawyer drafted a contract ensuring I would be informed of every thing to be modified, shot, and deleted with "due consideration given to my views." My next phone call was to the head of UTA. He'd called me on the set twice to show his support. But this phone call was not as comforting. He had already phoned my executive and told him, "Don't you realize you're killing this guy's career?!" The executive couldn't care less. I told my agent, "My lawyer drew up a contract stipulating that not a negative word would be uttered about me."

The agent laughed, "Are you kidding?! This guy is going to bad mouth you whether you fight him or not. Don't leave the job. They're going to fuck it up anyway. You might as well take your licks and avoid any stigma." I wish I had listened to him, but, at that point, I didn't know whom to trust.

I fired my manager/co-producer by letter that morning. My lawyer offered to do it, but I never shirked from something I needed done. The manager phoned my lawyer and said, "I had no choice but to side with the studio." My exec actually told the manager words I'd heard used before in jest: "If Rick doesn't step down, I'll bury him. He'll never work in this town again."

Holy shit! People actually said that. I thought it was a joke. It wasn't, but the guy who said it was. He was the nerd in everyone's high school, wreaking revenge on the world now that he finally had a smidge of control.

The Cheyenne saying "I ain't from around these parts" wasn't funny anymore. Doing a good job wasn't important here. I felt like a fish out of water, a babe in the woods, a chicken in the fox hole, the most naive bumpkin on the planet.

My line producer was rushing to mount a week of reshoots—new jokes to replace some of mine. Six of one, a half dozen of the other.

I received a phone call from one of the assistants I'd befriended. She was almost in tears, her hand covered the phone, and she spoke in a whisper. She told me, "Your manager has been on the phone all morning, phoning every studio exec and agent he knows, telling them he had to fire you and hire his other client to finish the film." Then she broke down crying. This was her first job. A rude awakening for me, shock and horror for her.

My lawyer tried to assuage me, "The last thing you want is to have some studio suit tell you what to shoot and how to shoot it." "I'm used to twenty suits giving me their opinion," I told him. "Doesn't mean I have to agree with them."

The reshoots were sent to me every day. This director was the biggest hack I'd ever seen. He never shot more than two takes and applauded after each one. It was all crap. Chudnow and my son and his partner watched them in disgust.

Then there was yet another preview—it was much shorter, which always helps. Just before the preview, we viewed the trailer, which included only scenes I'd directed. It was terrific! So we actually looked forward to the preview. The audience was the one I had cried out for: mostly male, between fourteen and twenty-four. They laughed a lot, But the cards at the end were worse than either of my first two previews. There was no ending in this version of the film—one of the primary reasons to hire the moron that directed the reshoots.

I stayed after the preview for the focus group, which, again, was worse than either of mine. I waited until the exec had his say and then unleashed a hurricane on him: "There is no ending. Half the jokes he replaced didn't get a murmur." He smirked, "I'm open to suggestion. Come up with an ending." I turned and, over my shoulder, muttered, "End this!" And I left.

Posters appeared on every billboard and bus bench in L.A., my name prominently displayed. My lawyer consoled me, saying, "This is going to open huge." I gave him an analogy: "What if your teenaged daughter, the light of your life, was all dressed in the finest designer clothes for the prom, bedecked in jewelry fit for a queen and advertised as the 'it girl,'" but only shortly after being irreparably brutalized by a horde of Orcs? That's what they did to me." And they were able to because I didn't listen to my inner maverick.

Spy Hard opened in third place behind ***Twister*** and ***Mission: Impossible***, ahead of ***Striptease***. It went on to gross over $27 million domestic in four weeks, competing against ***The Nutty Professor*** with Eddie Murphy, ***The Cable Guy*** with Jim Carrey, and ***The Rock*** with Sean Connery, directed by Michael Bay.

It opened number one at the box office in England, Germany, Italy, Spain, Brazil, Thailand, Venezuela, and Argentina, and it went on to gross over $86 million worldwide. And this was when tickets averaged five bucks instead of ten on 2000 screens instead of today's 4000.

The total projected gross for ***Spy Hard***, including pay and free TV and home video, is somewhere over $130 million on a budget of $20 million and a $15 million ad campaign. That's a lot of profit I'll never see. The studio sent me reports for the first two years. Each time the report displayed more income, the displayed costs were even higher, even though no additional money was spent. It's one thing to cook the books, but in this case, there must have been an entire cookbook with detailed recipes for frying, broiling, and baking the books.

To be a director, one has to have prettty thick skin. The least thing I learned, long after I left Cheyenne, was to have a nose for treachery. You really have to grow up and participate in this business from the time you're twelve to realize that *everyone* is out for themselves to an exponential degree more than in any other business. Well, there is always politics . . . the kind in government.

RULE # 30:

YOU'RE EITHER FUNNY OR YOU'RE NOT

Until a few years ago, comedies never won awards. Few receive positive critical reviews. I hold in the highest regard those performers, writers, and directors who endure the pain of comedy. Because no matter what classes in writing, acting, and directing you take, if you don't start out as a funny person, it's awfully hard to get laughs from strangers.

Chevy Chase told me he used to fall down and break his nose for twenty-five dollars a night. Then he did *Saturday Night Live*, and it became his signature. After getting millions of laughs for his pratfalls, his fancy managers and agents told him he was being too "broad." So he quit stumbling over things, and his career went into the toilet. Ten years later, Jim Carrey and even later, Jonah Hill and Kate McKinnon did the same physical comedy for tens of millions of dollars.

What's funny to some isn't funny to others. Find twelve people in any room, and half of them will differ in their opinion of what's funny. Most women hate the Three Stooges. Most men puke at saccharine romantic comedy. Most older folk cringe at explicit sex. Most teenagers won't see a movie without it. Here are some quotes about what is funny from my friend Dick Chudnow (his observations are totally subjective):

> Throwing a pie in someone's face is funny;
> throwing it up isn't.
>
> Farting at a wedding is funny;

farting in an elevator isn't.

You can sell even a bad joke if a fat man says it.

But what's the most important thing in comedy? ?

Timing!!!

That's because humor depends upon the situation, the character, the novelty of the joke, and a myriad of variables, including reactions and timing. My favorite humorless executive at Disney, when ordering me to shorten ***Spy Hard***, told me to delete scenes that were essential to the story. When I explained this problem, he answered, "Who cares?! Kids don't remember or care about the *story*!" I object: *Everyone* cares about the story. They want to know what's going to happen to characters in whom they've invested their time and emotion.

In *Easy Riders, Raging Bulls*, author Peter Biskind quotes directors who contend that the most important elements in a movie are the first five and last ten minutes. In comedies, the same holds true. Yet when creating a pitch or script for a comedy movie, additonal elements are equally important: the definition of the main characters and three to five set pieces that are examples of what these characters do that is funny.

Comedy might be one of the most difficult things to sustain in the world. Yoga masters have practiced holding off an orgasm for several hours. I bet those fuckers can't find a way to keep someone laughing for the same amount of time.

Comedy doesn't have to be mean nor demeaning, but it also doesn't have to be politically correct. If you touch on a nerve, and if it is a universal nerve people can identify with, they will laugh. Currently, in the early twenty-first century, the most common trend in comedy movies is having a "high concept"—a story that poses the question, "What if . . "

Historically, my favorite comedies poked fun at the cultural mores of the time. Religious stricture (who can forget Roberto Benigni's ***Life is Beautiful***—set in a concentration camp!); totalitarianism (Charlie Chaplin's ***The Great Dictator***); war (***Mash***); the pursuit of sex (***There's Something About Mary, When Harry Met Sally***, and ***American Pie***); crime (***A Fish Called Wanda, Bad Santa***, and ***Raising Arizona***); rascism and anti-semitism (***Get Out***, ***Inglorious Basterds*** and ***Django Unchained)*** and attempts at transgenderism (***Some Like it Hot, Tootsie, Victor Victoria***, and ***Shakespeare in Love***).

Remember: Studio executives don't take chances. In deference to these educated folks (who are probably relatives of other people in the biz), they all know their window of opportunity is limited. If they don't come up with a box office hit, they're out the door, so they all seek out scripts, writers, and comics who have had a box office hit. The MBA's who develop movies will only cast someone in a comedy role who's already been in a hit comedy movie or TV series because they've already gotten laughs.

I have experienced the kind of clout and power given to comedy stars twice. Once with Leslie Nielsen, as we sat across from Disney president Joe Roth, and once with Chevy Chase, as we sat across from former Warner president Mark Canton. Both of these actors are funny and have had multiple box office hit comedies. Without one of these stars, I would be swimming upstream. That's the way the comedy ball bounces. If some box office–proven comic says something, it is, by definition, funny.

* * * *

What has become manditory for comedy screenplays, before they are even shown to a comedy star, is a lengthy process of refinement. First a writer or writer duo sells a high-concept pitch or screenplay to a studio or production company. Then a series of development executives give their input about how to refine it. One studio executive was quoted in the *L.A. Times* as saying, "I don't feel I've done my job until I have a minimum of ten drafts of a screenplay, most times written by several different writers."

Good, funny ideas can come from anyone. As I've always told everyone I work with, if it's a good idea, I'll use it. Comedy requires free and open discussion—it's the best way to get the biggest laugh. But editing comedy is like walking on eggshells. My personal opinion, being an ex-editor and comedy director, follows the old Broadway adage: "Leave 'em wanting more." Sight gags that are surprising can be hysterical. But repeating the gag by cutting to it, then cutting to a reaction to it, and then cutting back to the gag is "milking the joke," and it negates its surprise.

Comedies are the most difficult type of movie to end. The plot is usually predictable because, if the concept is set up well, anyone with half a brain knows how it will end. We've all become used to and expect a happy ending in a comedy. This restriction—a happy, predictable ending—is in opposition to one of the most important elements of comedy: novelty. The unexpected is always funnier than the known. The only ending I found to be the funniest scene in the movie as the end credit sequence in ***The Hangover***.

In-your-face sophomoric comedies seem to be the most popular today in the early twenty-first century. They generally have formulaic plots with casts made of a fat guy, a nerd, and a guy having trouble attracting or keeping a woman. Thank goodness ***Bridesmaids*** at least used that same plot with women. Funny women.

There are dozens of classes in comedy writing in every major city. There are many improvisational comedy groups that run workshops in the major urban areas. There are countless ex-comics and currently unemployed comedy writers who give classes and lessons in comedy.

But as stated before, life lessons often teach you what you can't learn in school. The recent death of Robin Williams will be memorialized, psycho analyzed and editorialized ad infinitum. What will never be questioned is how incredibly naturally funny he was. As for the queen of sure-fire, off the cuff, barbs and hysterical bytes, Joan Rivers needed only the school of audience response to spur her on.

Sure, there's methods of delivery, physical comedy, and styles of writing that can be taught, but if you're funny and make people laugh in school, in the office, and in most places you inhabit, you're funny. Use it, dude; it's a godsent gift.

RULE # 31:

YOU CAN'T LEARN ANYTHING FROM ANYONE IN THE FUTURE, SO LEARN FROM YOUR FOREBEARS

During my childhood in Cheyenne, our movie theater showed cowboy movies and if you've seen one, you've seen 'em all. So it wasn't until later in life, after Arthur Knight's Monday Night at the Movies class at USC, that movies became my passion.

No one who doesn't work in movies can tell you what a director does. As quoted from the the Directors Guild of America's Minimum Basic Agreement, "The director is responsible for every element of the making of a motion picture." I believe that. But exercising this right is becoming more difficult every year. Writers and writer/producers in television treat directors as traffic cops. Movie studio executives find as many ways to get around the contractual limitations of staffing, fees, and minimum times required in pre-production, production, and post-production as possible.

At the time of this writing, there is no more hedge fund money for independent films. When money is tight, the bamboozlers come out of the woodwork. For comedy directors, there is an added element of pain. *Everyone* thinks they know what's funny. They don't, but they sure as hell think their viewpoint is more important than yours because they are paying you. What they forget is that they hired you because you have a background in writing and/or directing comedy and they don't. It would be like giving your dentist advice on filling a cavity.

Many of the comedy directors whose work I respect are also writers. In comedy, the script matters most because it describes the nuances of funny characters, situations that will elicit laughter, and dialogue that's humorous.

Casting comedic actors is essential to realizing a movie from a great comedy script. And the final element to enhance both of these is the director. Directors who have been comic actors or have written comedy films are the most capable of realizing a comedy movie. Most of the comedy directors I respect also wrote or co-wrote the movies they directed. I list them alphabetically here with the disclaimer that I have not liked all of their films, and that I have not listed other comedy directors whose films, albeit great commercial successes at the box office, weren't among my favorites. Here are my idols:

ROBERT ALTMAN: the master of orchestrating an ensemble of award-winning actors. My fav: ***Gosford Park***.

WES ANDERSON: a director/writer whose films display a novelty not found in mainstream films; a great example of this is ***The Royal Tenenbaums***. Even better, ***The Grand Budapest Hotel***.

The COEN BROTHERS have consistently come up with the most clever off-beat stories that treat violence as comedy. ***Raising Arizona***, ***Fargo***, and ***O Brother, Where Art Thou?*** are all gems.

TERRY GILLIAM directed my favorite Monty Python film, ***Monty Python and the Holy Grail***.

CHRISTOPHER GUEST, an improvisational actor, writer, and director, specializes in ensemble comedy. My fav: ***Best in Show***.

JOHN LANDIS directed ***Animal House, The Blues Brothers*** and ***Trading Places***, all winners.

BARRY LEVINSON wrote and directed the brilliant ***Tin Men*** and ***Diner***, which, according to *Vanity Fair*, is the progenitor of almost every "guy film" out today.

I've seen the above mentioned films many times. I may have subliminally copied elements or scenes from them all. Because I respect and have learned from my forebears. You should too.

RULE # 32

YOU NEED MORE THAN A GIRL AND A GUN

The esteemed French critic and film director, Jean-Luc Godard said, "All you need to make a movie is a girl and a gun." Here's a little more politically correct and specific modus operandi:

STEP ONE: You have an incredible screenplay (a *major* portion of the process.) But you have to attach an actor(s) that will obtain financing and distribution. The lower the budget, the better your chances. Movies that cost less than $ 5 million and an actor who means something to distributors, will allow you to proceed up the ladder to the next step. The three most important ingredients of making a movie: SCRIPT, CAST and NUMBER OF SHOOTING DAYS

The script has to have a great opening, a superb ending and some "set pieces" in between. The cast has to have actors you've auditioned that you *know* can carry off that script. The number of shooting days is one of the largest factors in determining the budget. If you don't have enough of them, you will not complete the film that's scripted. So modify the script to lose scenes, characters and locations that will not kill the story.

STEP TWO: Plan how to make your movie. The better you plan, the safer you'll be prepared to make a movie. Hire a seasoned, savvy, line producer. That's the person who knows whom to hire in technical positions and can negotiate their fees. The right person is as important in filmmaking as selecting the right spouse. In both cases you need someone who cares as much about your dream as you do.

Now hire a casting director. Your casting director must be someone who loves your script and comes in with ideas for people to cast even before you hire them because you like her/his ideas. With casting directors, it's not only their ideas that count, it's their relationship with talent agents and actors that may prove invaluable.

STEP THREE: Choose your cast, your key personnel and your locations. If only it was as easy as writing that one sentence. Always get recommendation(s) on whomever you hire. The nicest person in the world may not be the most competent. The most competent may be a major butt head. I'd take the latter over the former because your film requires the best support team you can get. After the film, you never have to see Mr. or Ms. Butt head again.

Making a movie is comparable to running a war. It's built on the military model of centralized command, troops responsible to their leaders and accountability dictated by these leaders. Here's a break down:

1. OFFICE STAFF: there is more paperwork in making a movie than is used in an Congressional inquiry. Script revisions, day-out-of-days reports (the shooting schedule), call sheets (who works where on each day), etc, etc. Fortunately everything's going electronic so that *everyone* will receive what used to be a mountain of paperwork on their iPads and cell phones. It will still require an entire office of production coordinators, production assistants, secretaries and drivers.

   LEARN THEIR NAMES.

   Not only will they, at some point in the movie, have your back, today's coordinator is tomorrow's producer, and whomever they work for in the future, they'll give their opinion of you.

2. KEY CREW: These are the captains, who will put your screenplay onto film or video. Director of Photography, Editor, Production Designer and Composer. They will all choose their staff and be in charge of them. Choose them well, respect their opinions and listen to their suggestions. You are the final authority, the General in this army, but your staff officers can either murder your film or make it live, sometimes better than you dreamed.

3. CAST: Casting is painful, but it is most important not to compromise. Make actors audition. Let them improvise. Ask them their thoughts on the character. Some of them have incredibly helpful suggestions that will make for a better film.

4. LOCATIONS (or sets): Remember that real estate mantra: location, location, location? Not only will this prove appropriate to the story, it will also give the actor's and, future audiences, comfort level of authenticity and artistry.

5. STORYBOARDS: Hire an experienced storyboard artist for those scenes which have stunts, special effects and action in them. This way, you have a common reference for every one on your team to ask questions pertinent to their involvement.

6. TECH SCOUT: Before you have a production meeting with the entire crew and go, page by page, through the script, it is important to take the script and the storyboards to every location so that each of your key personnel has in mind what they have to do to accommodate you.

STEP FOUR: Remember David Bowie's pep talk lyric, " This is ground control to major Tom, you've really made the grade." NOT YET. You better have a shot list made up for each day. You give a copy of that to the script supervisor and the assistant director and they will know how crazy you are. Be prepared to lose items from that list. Because....

THERE'S NEVER ENOUGH TIME.

Unlike Steven Spielberg, who re-shot the gigantic stunts for ***1941*** on a set of the Santa Monica pier several times, you will never pass this way again. Shoot what is absolutely necessary and know you have it shot. There are "hero" shots and there is "coverage." Establish the geography of where the scene takes place and give yourself choices of camera angles of the actors in the scene. Leave the "inserts," i.e. close shots of props for last. You can always fake them by shooting them elsewhere.

There is a rhythm to each shooting day and a rhythm to the overall shooting schedule. This is because it's a learning process for everyone. It's also because almost no film is shot in continuity – meaning in the order of the script. Due to locations, weather, actor availability, set construction and special effects, it just is not the most efficient manner in which to shoot a movie. So deal with it. Time is money and you don't have enough to shoot in continuity. Few people do.

You block out the first scene with the Director of Photography and Assistant Director who already pretty much know, from the tech scout, what's going to occur in this scene. You should rehearse the scene with the actors so that the Director of Photography can know what you have in mind for coverage and how to light it. Then send your actors back to finish their makeup and get dressed as the set/location is lit.

Shoot what you have in mind, adjust the dialogue if you need to, insure that you get enough camera angles (coverage) and, just when you you think it's five o'clock, the sun is going down and it's five minutes 'til seven when you have to wrap for the day. Drat! Why aren't you shooting in Norway in summer, where there's sun 'til Midnight?! For the same reason you chose to shoot this movie in Shreveport, Louisiana -- because you don't have enough money.

That's pretty much going to be the rhythm of every day except those days in which everyone knows there's a time constraint (remember the Bridge scene in Spyhard), that can't be overcome, so everyone must move in triple time. They will if, by that time, you have ingratiated yourself to the point of making them your family. When that point is reached, your crew and cast will walk over glass for you. Don't abuse that sentiment.

SOME DO'S AND DON'TS: Never talk down to anyone. Even your interns, who may be working for free. When dealing with actors, never give a line reading unless they ask you to. They believe they know how that character would talk.

Always plan your shots in one lighting direction. Finish all shots in that direction before you turn around and shoot the opposite direction. Jumping back and forth is extremely time consuming and unprofessional in the eyes of the crew.

Try to move locations/ set ups as little as possible. Again, time is money and the less you move, the less time you waste, especially when loading and unloading gear into trucks is involved.

Give praise when it's warranted. Both cast and crew want this movie to be as good as it can be. You are the KING/QUEEN and, as we've all learned, a benevolent leader is the one who keeps his/her head from being lopped off by a guillotine.

STEP FIVE: Post-production. Your new spouse, replacing your line producer, is your editor.. The old saying, "two heads are better than one" is not just meant for Siamese twins, it's meant for a Director and his/her Editor.

Give your editor the free rein to use her/his judgment. If you don't like what you see, exercise your right to change it. But do it diplomatically. You're going to be sitting in this room for a long time so you'd better be sensitive to your editor's feelings.

STEP SIX: Finishing touches include visual effects, additional sound recording (adding voices to crowd scenes that had no dialogue), sound effects (the most under-rated and important piece of the puzzle – just try watching a horror movie or a physical comedy without them,) sound mixing and color correcting.

The director is responsible for *all* elements of the making of a motion picture. Pay attention to every nuance. Ask questions about what your options are. Have them demonstrated to you. The people that work at these various crafts sometimes forget that you don't know what's possible and what's not.

STEP SEVEN: Previewing, advertising, interface with the distributor. Your film is finished and your Director's Guild contract has been exhausted. This is the most critical and difficult time to wield your power because you have none. After the contracted preview, you're just an unwanted appendage to a machine that has its own cogs and wheels.

Try to make friends with as many people in the areas of advertising and distribution as possible. Remember the ol' adage, "You can attract more flies with honey than vinegar" applies. The only leg you have up on them, provided they actually like your film, is that they hope that you may someday make great films and employ them in some capacity. Use this to your advantage. Praise them for their work if you like it. Be sensitive to criticizing their work, not them, if you don't. Above all, go to battle to insure you don't preview to the wrong audience!

Do whatever you have to do to get whatever you want. This ad campaign, this distribution plan is just another job for them. For you, it is the most important thing in your life.

RULE # 33:

NEVER REGRET DOING WHAT YOU'LL LATER REGRET NOT HAVING DONE

I'm reminded of Édith Piaf's iconic song: "*Je ne regrette rien*"—I have no regrets about coming to Hollywood even though everything that is real about Cheyenne is fake in Hollywood.

In Hollywood, marriages are for show (where do you think the term "trophy wife" emanated?) and status (the term "boy toy" could be a merit badge for the aging starlet), and they aren't expected to last. Marriages are comparable to the quote about not feeling fulfilled until ten rewrites of a script are written. Moguls and stars don't feel fulfilled 'til they've sampled the waters of whoever's younger, hotter, and looks better in photo ops.

It takes desire and maintenance to keep a marriage going. In Cheyenne, we kept our fences mended. In Hollywood, once a relationship is broken, it's permanent. Marriage and family in Hollywood matter much less than making that next movie.

I got a phone call from a soundman named David Nelson I worked with years ago when we shot documentaries. He was the ultimate techie and had hand made one of the first mobile telephones in L.A. With every job he did in the last of the '80s and early '90s, he bought another antenna atop Mount Wilson in Pasadena. These were repeater stations for the very first mobile phones before they went digital. He eventually sold them to L.A. Cellular for ten million dollars.

I came home from shooting the pilot of *The Real Housewives of Orange County* to a message from my wife, who said, "David Nelson called you." "David Nelson?! I haven't spoken to him in an eon!" I called the long-distance number he left, and when someone answered I began, "David?"

He laughed, "Do you know you may be the only person in Los Angeles with the same phone number you had ten years ago? I dialed you from memory—the one in my head." "David, not only do I have the same phone number, I still have the same house, the same wife, and the same kids who are no longer little toddlers."

No one in Hollywood stays with the same mate, partner, paramour, spouse, or children. It just doesn't fit in with the "they eat their young" model. But I'd never eat my young. I love 'em too much.

There is nothing I cherish more than the career I've chosen. It has enabled me to go places, meet people, and do things I'd never dreamt of being able to do. I've learned something on every single job I've done. Nothing has given me more fulfillment. I'll never lose the fascination with the craft. I'll never think I don't have more questions to ask. I'll never stop investigating any new technology or technique. I have yet to lose my dreams.

These days, when someone calls and says, "Let's have lunch," I'll ask 'em where and when.

POSTSCRIPT

I recently committed a maverick sin. I didn't follow Rule # 9: Never Get Your Hopes Up Higher than the Lowest Drawer in Your Desk. Once again, I did.

I reconnected with an old acquaintance. She is a warm, literate woman who had been the development person for Robert Redford's and Tom Cruise's companies. She was the person to first find and recommend ***Schindler's List***, which Cruise passed on—probably not Scientology sound or commercial enough.

I told her of a screenplay I have been trying to get financed for the past two years. It's a heist/chase comedy, a sort of ***Midnight Run*** meets ***The Italian Job***, and she wanted to read it. She read it in twenty-four hours and said she was going to give it to her producing partner. The partner read it in the next twenty-four hours. They phoned me the following day, the male partner promising he could get financing to make this movie. This may not sound unusual, but it is. Remember: No one reads. This was lightening-speed action, and it gave me hope.

Hope, in Hollywood, springs eternal. In my case the eternal means not sleeping at night, spinning out how the shots would look, who'd be perfect to cast, and how I'd carry off the end scene, which is a Mexican standoff à la ***True Romance***.

A meeting was set at a coffee shop centrally located to accommodate the three of us. We met to discuss what they had for a "battle plan."

After ***KGOD***, with critical reviews from the film festival and the industry people having seen it, I was courted by dozens of would-be or working producers. The first thing they do is buy you lunch at a trendy restaurant. Dinner would be too expensive, and they'd be unlikely to see other types like them, which is the reason for them to go to a trendy restaurant in the first place. The coffee shop this time was far from trendy.

In all the dozens of previous courtships I've had, the would-be producers paid for my meal. This time I paid for my own cappuccino. But, as I said, hope springs eternal . . . a short eternity, like one hour. After listening to all the things that they'd have to do to get this film financed, it was extremely difficult to act like I was listening. I'd heard it all before. Remember: *Everybody* in Hollywood has a script to sell. They wanted mine. For a long period of time with no option money.

My wife thinks I've mellowed. But actually, it's the reverse. I stopped the long-winded producer mid-sentence and said with obvious humor, "Ted (that's not his real name,) show me the money." With that, my old female acquaintance let out a gasp. I didn't think I was *that* rude. I was smiling and cordial.

But the gasp was because she noticed a parking enforcement officer writing a ticket to put on my windshield—she had seen me park in front. Normally, in these situations, just like people used to court you by buying you a meal, they'd also offer to pay your parking ticket and/or acknowledge their compassion for your plight with the Department of Motor Vehicles. But neither of these were forthcoming.

I got up and ran to beg the parking cop to let me off, but he'd already written the ticket. So I hopped in my car, scanned the fifty-five dollar ticket with rage, and drove off. Such is development hell, again. Why would I think it's changed?

Because, despite experience that should teach you differently, *you never know*. Today's windbag may be tomorrow's producer. So, even though I'm far too proactive to wait till tomorrow, something'll turn up . . .

Acknowledgements

To my wife, Laurel and my kids, Jason, Alix and Nick for not having me full time and hoping they're all stronger for it.

To my friend Dick Chudnow, for always answering the call to add funny.

To my literary and humane idol, Adriana Trigiani, author of *The Shoemaker's Wife,* the *Big Stone Gap* trilogies and a dozen more novels, for supporting and believing in my efforts.

To my friend, Melody Hessing-Lewis, PhD, author of *Up Chute Creek* for being my inspiration.

To Deborah Hocutt for the brilliant idea of making this a rule book and to Barrett Briske for wonderful copy editing.

To my longtime friend, Gino Tanasescu, for the brilliant cover.

To my friends Tony Cook and Erich Anderson for reading the first draft and making great suggestions without telling me how really bad it was.

To everyone who ever employed me, and you know who you are, thank you for taking a chance in a town that takes few chances.

To my dear uncle Norm for setting the example of how to be loved and respected.

To my brother, Dave, for coming from the darkness into the light and never losing his heart of gold.

ABOUT THE AUTHOR

Rick Friedberg is an award-winning writer/director of movies (***Spy Hard***), episodic TV (*CSI-Miami*), reality TV (*The Real Housewives of Orange County*), documentaries (*Rodeo Cowboy*), music videos ("Hot for Teacher"), and national and international TV commercials (shown during the Super Bowl, World Series, and NBA playoffs).

Visit his website: **http://www.rickfriedberg.com.**

ImDbpro: **https://pro-labs.imdb.com/name/nm0295007**

Facebook: **http://www.facebook.com/RickFriedberg**

LinkedIn: **https://www.linkedin.com/in/rickfriedberg/**

Twitter: **https://twitter.com/rickfriedberg**

YouTube: **http://www.youtube.com/user/rfriedb**

Vimeo: **https://vimeo.com/rickfriedberg1/videos**

For additional tips, anecdotes and humorous, insightful stories read my blog at: **http://HollywoodWarStories.com**

Printed in Great Britain
by Amazon

76818960R00118